Successful Techniques for Teaching Elementary Language Arts

Successful Techniques for Teaching Elementary Language Arts

ROSALIND MINOR ASHLEY

PARKER PUBLISHING COMPANY, INC. 016430
West Nyack, N.Y.

PRINTED IN THE UNITED STATES OF AMERICA
13-873752-5—B & P

DEDICATION

To my family, Chuck, Steve, and Rick Ashley,
and Fay and Jack Minor.

Why I Decided to Write This Book

The practical ideas in this book have resulted from working with children of different ages and backgrounds in three schools in two different school systems, each with different curricula; and exposure to a wide variety of educational materials. I served as Coordinator of Materials for one school, and had the opportunity to explore many new things. In addition, several farsighted and understanding administrators supported my efforts to experiment and innovate, and the bulk of this book is about my more successful experiments, with emphasis on individualizing instruction.

Motivating the pupil is of prime importance, and it is one of the main themes of this book. However, we should also look at the other side of the coin: many of the techniques which lead children to enjoy learning more will interest and excite the teacher as well! Everyone gets a lift from new, productive ways of doing things; for example, the new audio-visual equipment many of us are lucky enough to use. And there is much more than a novelty value in the use of the overhead projector. It really does improve instruction. I certainly never had a line of children waiting after school to practice handwriting before I used the overhead projector in my lessons. Another incentive to learning is an opportunity to tutor younger children.

There are also factors to avoid. For example, most teachers are so excited about individualizing instruction that it is important to keep the excitement under control. There is not much sense in teaching something separately twenty-six times that can effectively be taught to a group. However, in every subject area there are different specific skills needed by a few individuals. Why have everyone practice them? I believe in economy of effort, for the child as well as for the teacher, and actually, most of the best methods are not especially difficult.

Individualized Reading is not a panacea, but can be used as one of

7

three fine approaches to teaching reading, and should be coordinated with a specific system of follow-up activities and conferences. The book deals with many of the questions that come to the minds of teachers who have not tried Individualized Reading.

This book will also help you guard against an over-enthusiasm for independent work. It is an ideal, one worth working for, but it should not be rushed into. I am appalled at the thought of a teacher who is convinced an entire classroom can work independently on new concepts *with traditional materials,* and need little teacher help. Hidden under this delusion would be frightened, confused children guessing their way through new instructions and ideas, plus some lazy ones doing little or nothing at all. Until we can devise or buy programmed materials that will teach, explain, and reinforce completely, we must be wary of too much independent work with young children. In the interests of an overall presentation though, I will describe a few types of independent learning that have worked for me.

This book examines every important facet of language learning—and each item will be based on *real* classroom experiences. It covers ways to make use of the child's natural need to talk, and specific methods to focus attention and develop listening skill. It *is* possible to improve proofreading ability and composition without taking the creativity out of creative writing. I have included some of the new linguistic methods I've used to teach grammar in an interesting way, as well as some keys to individualizing spelling, and ways to keep oral reading fun. The ideas have worked with my pupils and have made teaching an even more joyful experience.

R.M.A.

Acknowledgments

I am grateful for the help and suggestions given by Steve, Chuck, and Rick Ashley; Fay and Jack Minor; Dr. William J. Attea, Director of Instructional Services, District 39, Wilmette, Illinois; William J. Fritsche, Director of Curriculum, District 39, Wilmette, Illinois; Loretta Doyle, National College of Education; Robert L. Hillerich, Assistant Superintendent of Schools, Glenview, Illinois; Joyce Arkin, Weber Elementary School, Parkway School District, Creve Coeur, Missouri; Renata Morse, Milwaukee, Wisconsin; Margo Turner, Roberta Goldstein, Tamra Schubert, and Mary Dinkel, of Romona School, District 39, Wilmette, Illinois; Betty Kelly, Librarian, Instructional Materials Center, District 39, Wilmette, Illinois; Peggy Pressley, Glenview, Illinois; Elise Gieser, Harper School, District 39, Wilmette, Illinois; and Linda Fischer, Howard and Locust Junior Highs, District 39, Wilmette, Illinois. I am also grateful to Harold Smith, Principal, Romona School, District 39, Wilmette, Illinois; Winifred Overstreet, Evanston, Illinois; Dr. Robert D. Hartman, Superintendent of Schools, Carmel, Indiana; Margaret Erb, former Principal of Harper School, District 39, Wilmette, Illinois; Dr. Donald V. Grote, Superintendent of Schools, District 39, Wilmette, Illinois; and Donna Secrist, Librarian, Willard School, District 65, Evanston, Illinois; all of whom have given help, encouragement, and freedom to experiment in my teaching career, making this book possible.

9

Contents

     WRITING FUN 162

     The First Steps in Introducing Cursive Writing   162
     Earn Your Name Card   167
     Use Lined Color Transparencies   168
     How to Cope with Eager After-School Practicing   169
     "How Am I Doing?"—Self-Evaluation   170
     What to Do if They're Practicing Incorrectly   171
     Kinesthetic Methods   171
     Motivation and Attention   172
     Individualization   172
     Something New   172

12. HOW TO KEEP ORAL READING FROM BEING A BORE   174

     The Conference Method   175
     Reading to Younger Children   175
     Say Now, Play Later—Using the Tape Recorder   176
          *To Avoid Embarrassment. Procedure. Don't Overdo It.
          Playback.*
     How to Find Time for Oral Reading—Combine It with Art,
     Literature, and Social Studies   178
          *Reading Follow-ups. Choral Reading. Plays for Reading
          Aloud. Dramatized Radio or Television Broadcasts. Sug-
          gestions.*
     Why Is a Rehearsal Better Than a Lesson?   185
          The Question. The Answer.

13. DEVELOPING A COMPLETE READING PROGRAM 188

     Three Complementary Approaches to a Varied Reading Pro-
     gram   189
          *Is Individualized Reading Enough? Basic Readers—In-
          dividualized Approach. Grouping.*
     Individualized Reading   192
          Reading Laboratories for Independent Work.
     Try Varied Reading Materials   192
     Group Versus Individual Phonics   193
     Can Some Reading Group Lessons Be Tape Recorded?   193
     Shall We Scrap the Basic Reader?   194
     Teaching Aids   195
     Correlate Reading with Other Curriculum Areas   196
     Project to Help Disadvantaged Children   197
     Changes in School Libraries   198

Successful Techniques for Teaching Elementary Language Arts

1

Keys to Stimulating Pupils' Interest in Using Language Arts

The little girl glared at me as I waited. She had something to say about my question, so she groped for words, and complained, "You've got the answers in *your* book."

This book too has answers. One question might be, "How can we relax and enjoy teaching while we motivate children to use language?" Teaching, at its best, is fun for the teacher. Pupils sense and share the enthusiasm. How do teachers reach mutual enjoyment and achievement? Let's let pupils do "what comes naturally" at times. While it is true that there are many problems, it is also true that we can try to prevent them.

The angry little girl with the answerless book was right. It *is* easier for the teacher, who is always so glad later when she hasn't rushed a child. The pat answer comes quickly, often with no thought. Children need time to think, and a thoughtful analysis expressed in the right words is worth waiting for.

There are other urgent needs. Activities will be planned that utilize a pupil's natural talkativeness. All people love to try out new equipment, but children most of all. Let's lure them into learning with gadgets, hoping that pupils will get interested and start learning for the joy of it. Youngsters also need to feel that they are useful. Utilize this by encouraging them to work with others rather than to compete with them.

You'll share experiences with pupil tutoring, an exciting new approach to learning. Older children, stimulated by the responsibility of teaching lessons, suddenly began to put more time and effort into their work. It seemed that the tutors received as much as they gave. Their young pupils' questions put the tutors on the spot. This challenge resulted in learning for both age groups.

Deal directly with the problem of the pupil who dislikes language work. Show him that it isn't boring.

New experiments in composition with very young primary children are leading the way to earlier competency in oral and written expression.

Let's also delve into the subtleties of mystery, and "play detective" while children practice using the parts of speech, or word classes.

Problems We Must Meet

Teachers must cope with problems in teaching language arts, as in all subjects. Many of them are difficult to solve, and will not be resolved by using a game or an imaginative idea. Even an enthusiastic teacher cannot move mountains. A child who is physically or mentally sick is unable to learn at times. When a pupil comes from a broken home he is not always interested in school work. There are many individual differences in intelligence, motivation, and attention span which can cause learning problems for pupils. Every subject has facets which are less enjoyable to children than others. You've all heard a group groan at one time or another. However, interesting activities can fight a brave battle against learning difficulties caused by low intelligence, boredom with previous school experiences, inattention, poor listening habits, and general sluggishness.

This book will try to solve some of your teaching problems, but it does not claim to help them all. Its main function is to prevent many problems through motivation and attention to individual differences.

How to Channel Natural Needs into Learning Experiences

Each child feels the need to think things out, to talk, to explore, to be helpful, to feel accepted and important. It's our job to make use of these drives, exploiting them so that the pupil uses and practices language, improving his skills while he satisfies deep cravings.

Need to Think

Perhaps teachers should try to achieve a better balance between their activities. A child cannot absorb information all day. He needs an opportunity to mull over what has been fed into his mind, to distill it, and to express his own opinions on it. In the rush to cover material do educators allow this time for creation? The deep satisfaction a child will show makes up for the time spent. The goal is not memorized facts, but the ideas and judgments which should come from the facts.

Need to Talk

Since, for much of the school day, a pupil must inhibit his desire to speak, let's make a real learning activity out of it when he does talk. It is a natural resource to be treasured, not stifled. By channeling speech into stimulating discussions, buzz sessions, and conversation games, teachers can drain away the need for chatter during quiet study time. Of course, it takes some skill to tactfully keep the orator brief and on the subject, but this is needed too. Plan some oral activities for each day.

Need to Explore New Media

You might feel that it's out of your reach to dream of motivating children with the new audiovisual equipment used by many teachers. Don't be discouraged if your district doesn't provide each classroom with a tape recorder, overhead projector, television set, record player, filmstrip previewers, and study carrels. Most don't, because of the cost. Be aggressive and sign up for everything you need that you can get at your Instructional Materials Center or library. You may be amazed at the variety of equipment you'll be able to borrow for two to four weeks at a time. If you show administrators that you'll use this educational hardware, your chances of getting some of your own in the future will be greatly improved.

Every child is originally curious about books, but we dull this by their over-use. Vary the educational diet of your class with pictures, filmstrips, films, educational television, and programmed books.

A completely new concept in language teaching for fifth-grade and above is the *Labacus,** one of 30 sentence-making plastic devices in

---

* Laidlaw Brothers (a Division of Doubleday and Co., Inc.), River Forest, Ill.

The Laidlaw Linguistic Laboratory. It permits pupils to manipulate their language physically as well as mentally, and to see the structure of a sentence.

USE OF FILMSTRIPS

If you can't keep a filmstrip previewer available in your corner for enrichment, try borrowing one. Another idea is to try to make arrangements with your librarian to send pairs of children in to the library to see pre-selected filmstrips. Pupils may be tired of reading their chapter, but this is a new way of learning the same ideas. It is also another approach for the learner with a short attention span, or for one who speaks little English. The child who gets bogged down on written work may be a ball of fire when he knows he may see a filmstrip if he finishes. There are excellent ones available on phonics, spelling, and dictionary skills, as well as on children's literature.

Use of Overhead Projector

The overhead projector is a tool for the teacher and a delight for pupils. Try to prevent the learning of cursive writing from becoming drudgery by allowing individuals to practice on the overhead projector. A child can write for every one to see. It's a good idea to allow volunteers to demonstrate handwriting, fill in missing answers on transparencies, and to conduct their own prepared lessons using the lightboard. You can guess why a youngster will put so much of himself into his own lesson. Even a lazy one can be inspired by the responsibility of a topic, an assigned date and time written in the teacher's plan book, and free use of the overhead projector to teach his classmates. The reason? There are at least two:

1. The lesson is his own, not the teacher's.
2. He enjoys using a new thing. His writing and sketches will appear magically on a screen.

Use of Teletraining Equipment

Have you made use of the free audiovisual materials available for borrowing? A very fine teaching aid for language experience is provided free by most local telephone companies. Contact your local business office for information on what is available in your area. One teletraining series consists of practice telephone equipment, a motion picture, four filmstrips, three wall charts, a pupil's booklet with a place for alphabetizing names with phone numbers, and a teacher's guide with many excellent ideas.

The importance and history of communication, courtesy, and the science of sound are taught in this series. One filmstrip is called "The Alphabet Works for Us," and was designed to supplement classroom study, offering extensive alphabetizing practice, so that children will be able to use telephone directories.

The Teletrainer, containing two training telephones, is used to develop skills in oral communication through actual demonstration in practice conversations. With it you can teach lessons in projecting a pleasing personality with your voice, handling situations by telephone (including emergencies), and role-playing materials and tests. The teacher's manual offers practical guidance in taking messages, inquiring, informing, persuading, and exchanging ideas over the telephone. Library copies of an 83-page booklet, "Mr. Bell Invents the Telephone," part of the Landmark Series, are also provided.

Use of Films

Some free color films which are provided in most areas by local telephone companies are called "Science Behind Speech," and "Alphabet Conspiracy."

If you do not use films as often as you'd like to, because of their unavailability or limited selection, investigate the companies which offer free films for school use. One company offers a small catalog called "The Modern Index and Guide to Free-Loan Educational Films for Schools." You can obtain free 16-millimeter films by filling out an order form or writing a letter. The films are sent to you postage free, and you pay return postage only.*

Another firm offers a large catalog with a listing and topical guide for free films. The films are ordered from the branch office nearest to you.†

Use films for the excellent discussion possibilities they offer. Language opportunities are developed, no matter what subject you

---

* Modern Talking Picture Service, 1212 Avenue of the Americas, New York, N. Y. 10036.

† Association Films, Inc., 347 Madison Ave., New York, N. Y. 10017.

discuss. No child can resist giving his opinions after viewing a film. All he needs is something interesting to stimulate him.

Use of Posters

Make it a learning experience even when a child gazes around the room, as each one will at times. Have word cards posted on appropriate walls, saying *north, south, east,* and *west.* Keep distracting exhibits and posters in the back.

Tie words in with all subject areas. Always have a few words on the chalkboard related to science or mathematics. An interesting safety or health poster can be hanging on another wall.

Vary your lessons whenever you can by using the many audiovisual aids available to you.

WHO'S TEACHING WHOM?—PUPIL TUTORS

In the past educators have mistakenly labeled a child's wish to help others as cheating. Perhaps there is a little of that, but let's use this instinct for sharing to stimulate positive experiences in spelling, handwriting, discussions, and all other language study, having pupils work as partners, committee members, and teams. Social living cannot be isolated from language activities. True education assimilates practice in working with others into each curriculum area.

Tutors for Younger Pupils in Other Classes

Arrangements can be made with another teacher in your school to have your pupils tutor hers. Many very happy experiences resulted when some fourth-graders taught small groups and individuals in a second grade.*

The obvious question that comes to mind about the new experiments in pupil tutoring is, "What about the work the tutors miss?" This question will no longer bother you after you analyze the values inherent in the tutoring. In a traditionally set up classroom, work can be made up easily by superior and average pupils. Slow learners will find that it's worth the extra homework to be able to tutor others. However, now that many classes are organized into small group

---

* Mary Dinkel, Rosalind Ashley, Romona School, District No. 39, Wilmette, Ill.

and individual independent learners, there is an opportunity for those who need it most to do the tutoring as one of their regular activities, without falling behind. Even the slowest child feels the urge to have a turn when others are chosen to be tutors. This pupil will probably gain more than any other. His ego is involved, and how does he react to the prospect of teaching reading, spelling, or grammar to a younger child? The previously unmotivated prospective tutor takes his book home and studies it so he won't be embarrassed before his younger pupils the next day. He will get a glint in his eye when you suggest that he prepare questions to ask after a reading lesson. To write and answer these questions he'll have to know this story inside out, but suddenly he doesn't mind. He has always been unwilling or forgetful about taking his book home before. What caused the change? There's a new reason for effort. He's going to *use* the story. The increased comprehension and organizing skill gained from this more than make up for the half hour away from your class or from his other assignments. Aside from that, add up the voluntary time spent at home preparing his lesson. Many times you can suggest tutoring lessons from the tutor's own basic reader, so that no time at all will be lost from his own textbook progress.

Another plus value for this type of tutoring is the fact that it's contagious. You don't have to force it—just sign them up. It's amazing what children will volunteer for—they will try just about anything!

Pupil Teachers for
Contemporaries in Other Classes

A different form of tutoring by fellow pupils was tried between two fourth grades, to their mutual advantage. One group had completed a science unit on "The Human Body." The other class was about to begin this study, but was a little short on time to go into it deeply. Arrangements were made between the two teachers for small groups of children who had finished the unit to come in to teach it to their peers, using the charts, diagrams, and transparencies they had prepared themselves. Cross-sectioned, full-sized models of the human body, with removable organs, were used. The children did a remarkable job of presenting the basic facts, showing the organs, labeling the diagrams, and then answering questions from the floor. Their audience was spellbound, not only by the awesome subject and models, but by the skillful oral presentation. The pupil teachers were stimulated to exert their best efforts by the eagerness and perceptive questions of the audience. These speakers overstayed their allotted time by popular request of class and teacher, and enjoyed their triumph so thoroughly that they asked to return one day sooner than scheduled. Obviously, this responsibility, plus the opportunity to demonstrate their visual materials, was a thrilling impetus to further achievement in science and language.*

Pupil Tutors within One Class

Fascinating experiments are now under way in many districts, trying out multi-age groupings, which deliberately place youngsters together who may be as much as three years apart in age.† Grade labels are discarded in favor of the idea of continuous progress. The resulting difference in skills in one classroom leads naturally to informal helping and formal tutoring. Great social benefits can be achieved, so that children learn more than the curriculum by teaching and learning together.

SUGGESTIONS FOR STIMULATING THE CHILD WHO HATES LANGUAGE WORK

Use of Science Experiments

Use offbeat ideas and other subject areas to try to convince a child that he doesn't hate language study. The best approach is to use as a starting point experiences he enjoys. The pupil who thinks he hates language lessons will respond to the fun of a science experiment. When he sees the results of these experiments, he will be eager to share them with the group. This child will beg to tell the class about it. He can be encouraged to take short notes, write simple reports, and keep charts on the chalkboard. He will be eager to write the results as he gets them, because he sees a *need* for writing. How else will everyone know what happened? Written records make sense as a way of reporting important experiences. To keep interest high, don't insist on having all experiments written up. The most exciting

---

* Tamra Schubert, Rosalind Ashley, Romona School, District No. 39, Wilmette, Ill.

† Romona School, District No. 39, Wilmette, Ill.

way for him is to show his equipment, tell what he hoped to accomplish, and demonstrate his results orally.

Use of Group Evaluation in Creative Writing

By recording an informal discussion of a child's story you can interest a group in improving their language skills. After a few stories have been discussed, play the tape back, listen to what has been said, talk about the stories and the comments on them, and evaluate each other's efforts. Aim for objective, helpful criticism which can lead to better stories, not hurt feelings. Encourage pupils to look for good points as well as flaws.

Use of Teacher as Private Secretary

If you have a pupil who sits with a blank paper in front of him, just staring at it and obviously unable to make a start, the situation needs your help. One effective solution is to suggest a conference. If the child is trying to write a story you can say, "I'll help you. Let's write this together. I know you have some good ideas. Tell me about them." As the child begins to talk, write down his words and read them back to him. You might say, "You wrote your story already. Here it is!" By then he'll probably be bursting with ideas on how to change it and improve it, but it's easy for him now, as it's already written. Accept it as it is. Praise the good things in it. A little success sparks more ideas, and still more. If there are mistakes, save them for later. The precious creation must be valued, and new ideas preserved before they're forgotten. You will be much more patient if you think of *your* weakest subject, and how much you'd like a little start in it once in a while.

Use of Starters

You'll find a day when nothing works. You ask a child to tell you his thoughts, and he has none. Even when he tries, there's nothing. He's not even interested in his interests. Don't give up. Perhaps there will be an idea for you in this experience:

The boy just sat there.

"I can't think of anything," he said.

"I'll give you a beginning," I answered.

He looked happier. "Okay."

I gave him the beginning. "Once upon a time . . . "

We both laughed. "Thanks for nothing," he replied.

"All right. Try this. Once upon a time there was a magician."

"Okay," he said again, and he went to his seat. I didn't expect anything.

The next morning he handed in one long, sloppy paragraph.

"Here's my story," he beamed. "That was a great first line you gave me."

We corrected his mistakes a few days later. No matter how short or how ordinary his paragraph was, it was creative to *him*. To correct it too soon might have stifled his creativity.

The story was acceptable. Sometimes we have to settle for less.

CURRENT EXPERIMENTS TO HELP
FIRST GRADERS ENJOY COMPOSITION

The very young and the very reluctant writers will both benefit from telling their stories or experiences, using a tape recorder. When they hear the tape played back it is much easier for them to copy it down as written language. Some first grades use this method with great success, leading the pupils to better independent written composition.*

USE OF MYSTERY TO INTEREST PUPILS
IN PARTS OF SPEECH

Everyone loves a secret or a riddle. Use a child's natural curiosity and enjoyment of role-playing to teach grammar. Have the class pretend to be detectives. Solve the mystery of a missing noun or verb. Summarize lessons with a bulletin board or a visual using this title, "Be a Detective. Find the Missing Noun." Draw question marks, magnifying glasses, footprints, or Sherlock Holmes hats around the border. The lesson with the blank for the missing part of speech will be more interesting.

USE OF DRAMA, HUMOR, AND ANTICIPATION

Don't ever hesitate to be corny if the children like it. Be dramatic! If "all the world's a stage," *you're* on it. Ham it up, and feel your little audience respond as they never have before. Children react well to

---

* Central School, District No. 65, Evanston, Illinois.

surprises, jokes, and unusual approaches. They may be a captive audience, but their attention is elusive. Try a few tricks once in a while. They even enjoy the ones that don't quite come off. Pupils listen, if for no other reason than that they are curious to find out what you're up to. Always have an exciting plan ahead, whether it's a mural you're starting, a trip the class is looking forward to, a newspaper you're preparing, a resource person coming for a visit, or a puppet show you're rehearsing. There is a very fine line between play and work. It's a lucky group that hurries to school to find out what the plans are for the day. In an atmosphere of expectant enjoyment each child is bursting with energy to accomplish something. Having fun guarantees attention; a learning experience doesn't have to be painful to be good.

CHECKLIST

Prevent many learning problems by fresh, new activities that capture attention.

Give each child time to think and create.

Utilize the pupil's natural need to talk by planning some oral activities each day.

Lure children into using language by having equipment of all kinds available.

Beg and borrow equipment which your district cannot buy for each teacher.

Vary your lessons as much as you can. You don't like to do the same thing all the time either.

Promise and provide enjoyable future experiences to keep slow or motionless workers moving.

Explore all available possibilities of films, educational television, demonstration equipment, trips, and resource people.

Teach social living by encouraging committee work and studying with partners.

Pupil tutoring works better than many methods. Try it.

Don't desert your slow or reluctant workers. Give them a little push to help them start.

Tape record stories for children who are unable to write them on paper, or allow them to tell the stories to you.

Correct all mistakes in stories, but don't deaden creativity by doing it too soon.

Use mystery, drama, and humor to stimulate interest.

Try to keep an experimental, fun-loving attitude toward your work, varying it all the time by planning *big* projects and events. Enthusiasm is catching.

2

Let Them Talk – Ways to Use Oral Language in Learning Experiences

Here are some special activities that combine oral language with many other curriculum areas, which can result in young people not only knowing how to speak effectively, but also having something worthwhile to say. Each day presents its share of opportunities to make speaking meaningful and a way of growing. Are we wasting or missing them entirely?

Some of the best chances occur in bad weather, when children must stay indoors and still have a break in their studies. You should look forward to these moments instead of dreading them. Along with precious extra time for developing language skills, you have an informal chance to communicate with and strengthen your rapport with the young individuals in your care. There will never be a child who has nothing to say if he is encouraged, praised for his efforts, and reminded of things he likes to do when he needs ideas. Certainly, we must never allow one pupil to have too much to say at the expense of the others. There are many diverting ways of guiding children to oral fluency and self control.

A WAY TO COMBINE ORAL LANGUAGE
WITH ENTHUSIASM, SOCIAL STUDIES,
SCIENCE, READING, HEALTH AND SAFETY

What better way can there be to start a day than with the news that pupils are eager to tell anyhow? We may *call* it Current Events, but this period so rich in interest, close attention, and enthusiasm is training in an endless list of skills, as well as an opportunity for uncovering boundless information on past events, speculating about future events, and using a time line to pinpoint past and current history in time.

Teach Social Studies

Try to allow a few minutes in your morning news-sharing to orient your children in space, as well as in time. Use the golden chance to pull down the map and find the country or city you're all speaking about. Let a child point to a place on the globe, while another tells his news item. Geography can only be *made* dull—it's as exciting as travel. Does a child use Current Events time to discuss a past or future trip? This is the geography that means something to him. Let him find and show the place on the map. It's also an excellent way of cutting him short politely.

There are so many adults who are unconcerned about local, national, and world news events that you feel you are making a rare contribution when you interest children in reading newspapers and listening to news programs. They will become better citizens and more well-rounded people if they are really aware of the world they live in. A child who begins by reading comics may move up to sports columns, reviews, and editorials later. Never despair over the apparent trash children seem to prefer to the educational items. They're building a newspaper habit, and they'll become better-educated people who have something interesting to say on many topics. The reading of newspapers will strengthen their vocabularies, as well as widen the scope of their conversation and ideas. It's reading practice, just as much as that done in their basic readers; and it's done on their own time!

Teach Health

What do you do when someone has a choice tidbit he has read about a new cure or strange disease? Do you cut off the lively conversation just as a few people want to share some of *their* symptoms? No—tie it in to something you want them to know about health habits. A rule or fact that is part of a pattern will be recalled more easily than a bit of isolated health information.

Teach Safety

Does your group thrive on discussing gory accidents? It's a human failing. You can change the subject by relating the accident to safety precautions we should all take. Pupils may remember it better because they associate the lesson with something exciting to them.

If you're the typical busy teacher, you're probably saying that this sounds fine, but we all know that there'd be no time for reading lessons if we had Current Events every day. Do it as often as possible. Even three times a week for 20 minute periods will be valuable. To still your conscience, write it in your plan book as "Language *and* Social Studies." The occasional science, health, and safety discussions will be like a bonus. They can't be planned. Use the news as it comes. Of course, weather is always news, because it affects our lives so intimately, so extend the short weather items to your weather and climate ideas in science and social studies.

To avoid frustration on the child's part when he brings in a news item to share and no time is available to hear it, it's a good idea to save one corner of your bulletin board for current events. Let the child staple up his article himself, and urge everyone to read it. This will keep the class newspaper-conscious each day, whether a current events discussion is allowed time or not.

But Can They Read a Newspaper?

You may wonder what age child is able to read a difficult adult newspaper. Don't limit yourself or your pupils. Urge them to read what they can, discuss it and get help from their parents, and consult you about words and names. The very best reports are made in a child's own words. The absolutely worst ones are articles read directly from the newspaper, as the pupil stumbles over difficult words he knows nothing about. Newspaper reading is a skill which can be achieved gradually, so don't worry about the reading level. This seems to jump when children *want* to know something. Items about astronauts are usually easier for them. Some eight-year olds will do well on many parts of a newspaper, and other eleven-year olds will struggle with most of it. Not all of those in a group will be able to participate fully in the sense that they have read a newspaper well, but they will benefit in proportion to how much of it they have read. Even the child who finds it too difficult to read it at all will receive fringe benefits from this activity. The discussion leads him to want to know more about the news of the world, and radio and television will keep him up on things, so he can join in and give his oral items too.

ARE WE MISSING LANGUAGE OPPORTUNITIES?

Book Sharing

Are you in a rut—assigning written book reports for each book read It's time to climb out and vary your reading activities. For example, try book sharing. It's an oral teaser which tells just enough of the plot to sell a book to the child's classmates. The title and author of the book can be written on the board, and slips of paper passed out to those interested in copying down the information, so that they can obtain and read the story.

Chalk Talks

Chalk talks are also great fun, as children love to work with partners. They can plan ahead to read the same book, and sign up for a special date and time when they will present the chalk talk to the group. When the partners have finished reading their books, they work together on the chalk talk as a team. One tells about part of the story, while the other makes quick line drawings on the board with colored chalk. This can also be done on an overhead projector, writing on a transparency with colored pens. Halfway in their presentation the pupils will wish to switch parts, and the one who was talking may now draw, while his partner finishes the oral talk. Private practice opportunities are essential for an effective chalk talk. Chalk talks are enjoyable, even when the artist can't keep up with the speaker. In fact, this type of occurrence can add a lot of humor to the proceedings. Remind the speakers to stop and wait once in a while. The performers may not sell their particular book, but just about everyone will want to do a chalk talk after they see and hear the first one.

Creative Dramatics

Have you investigated the possibilities in creative dramatics? The oral language practice, the freedom of expression, and the creative potential inherent in this activity make it a must for you to try. You can introduce dramatics by allowing a small group to dramatize part of a book. Don't let the fact that the children think it's play fool you. They're really learning.

Science Demonstration

A combination microprojector demonstration and talk could be presented by two able pupils. This will require advance preparation, but it is a way of sharing your microscope findings with the group and discussing them together.

DISCUSSIONS

Prepare pupils to have intelligent discussions by demonstrating that they are much more than just talk. Define the main duties of a discussion leader:

1. Present or develop problem.
2. Keep group on subject.
3. Summarize within and at the end of discussion.
4. Help to resolve problem by vote or consensus.

Every member needs to be involved in a good discussion and should help the group arrive at a democratic decision. Explain that participants as well as leaders have responsibilities. They must be willing to make some preparation, and to evaluate their evidence for reliability. Participants must cooperate by contributing, listening, and attempting to keep to the discussion topic.

Have a Classroom Club

The best device for encouraging and practicing oral expression can be a classroom organization or club. Most nine- or ten-year olds are able to function fairly well as officers or members.

Getting Started

The first step in achieving an orderly, democratically set up group is to ask the class if they want a club, and to allow them to vote on it. They will certainly vote to have one, so allow a meeting time in your plan book one afternoon a week. The last 20-minute period of the day is an appropriate time slot for a relaxed oral activity like this. Conduct the first meeting yourself, without minutes. Take nominations from the floor, have them seconded, and allow the class to vote for a slate of officers. A president, vice-president, and secretary are usually enough for your executive board. Allow at least two weeks for campaigning with posters and speeches, and then have the election. Do not turn the meeting over to them yet. It's better that they first have help in preparing for their responsibilities. The officers will grow into these jobs if you show them the way. A good starter is a book called, *So You Were Elected,* by Virginia Bailard.* Depending on the age of your officers, plan how much of the book they should read, as it's difficult reading. Mark the suggested pages with paper clips at the start and finish. Be sure to help pupils with the book if it is hard for them to read. Have the president read it first, pass it on to the vice-president, and then the secretary. Keep the book available to other class members later, in case they'd like to read about parliamentary procedures and the duties of officers. This book will teach methods of running an organization and the rules of order. It will give the officers clues on attaining the dignity needed to command attention and respect from their peers in order to accomplish class business in an efficient manner. Skip some procedures for younger pupils.

Board Meetings

The three class officers should meet with you for a board meeting before class one day, in order to prepare a simple agenda, or plan, for their first meeting. They'll need some guidance in order to get started, but try to listen more than talk. Enter into their meeting when asked for advice, or if the officers get off the subject. If, in the beginning, they have no idea at all of what kind of business a class club should have, be ready with some suggestions for them. It may seem that you're exploiting your class, but when they need ideas, they'll be glad to accomplish things and have discussions and voting for you that you were going to do yourself anyway, saving on lesson time. Here are a few suggestions for possible discussion topics for a class organization agenda. They would be suitable for third-graders, or for older children.

1. Decide what game or activity the class wishes for the next rainy day recess.

---

* New York, McGraw-Hill Book Co., Inc., 1966.

2. Choose a class motto or emblem or secret name to post on our door.
3. Plan for the next free time period when a birthday party is scheduled.
4. Vote on a follow-up activity for the next field trip, to make the trip more meaningful.
5. When it's time for a mural, (about November), have the class decide which social studies unit they wish to summarize in the mural. You can't wait too long to begin, as the planning and art work are very time-consuming.
6. Discuss behavior in the halls and cafeteria.
7. Ask the group whether they'd like to have a monthly newspaper or magazine, to publish their writing and art work.
8. If a newspaper or magazine is planned, vote on a name for it.

If the class wants a newspaper or magazine, select the editors yourself. Give anyone a chance, not just the popular people, or those who get good marks all of the time. They're not the ones who need it most. If you have slow students for editors, your paper may not be great, but the editors will grow in many ways from the experience. Keep your goals in mind. The editors will choose from volunteers for their staff.

The above suggestions are enough for many agendas, but your officers may need ideas more than once.

As you can see, there are many items of business suitable for the class to handle. A well-run club teaches children how to live with each other in a civilized way. Each pupil will learn that the majority's wishes must be respected, and the group as a whole will keep malcontents in line, and perhaps win them over.

GAMES

Send a Message

Do you know any story-telling games?

One game that is always hilarious is called *Send a Message*. Divide the class into two teams of equal size, lined up on opposite sides of the room.

Write up identical messages ahead of time, seal them in envelopes, and give them to the first member of each side. At a signal, the first contestant on each side tears open the envelopes, reads the messages, and tears them up. After this, they turn and whisper the messages into the ears of the pupils behind them. Those people turn and whisper the message to those behind them. This continues until the messages have gone through each line to the last person on each side. These last pupils then run to the judge and tell him the message. To make the judging easier, the judge should write down this last message from each side. The winning team will be the one which delivers the most accurate message, not the one that finishes first. To make it more difficult, choose a message that's hard to say, although it's best not to have more than ten words. A good, hard message for elementary pupils might be, "Aunt Effie's irritated esophagus has shown improvement after extended treatment." You could simplify it for primary groups. An important side value, besides the language practice and enjoyment, is the experience of seeing how a message gets distorted in transmission, an important lesson for daily living.

One game for elementary pupils which eliminates players quickly involves fast thinking and spelling. It's called *E,* and is based on the fact that the letter *E* is used more often than any other letter in the alphabet. Tell the class this fact when you explain the game. Ask a series of questions of the pupils as they stand in line. Change the questions once in a while. The questions may have the letter *E* in them, but the answers may not. Appoint a timekeeper, and allow no more than 20 seconds for each answer. Any child who uses a word containing the letter *E* in his answer, or who cannot answer within the time limit, is out. The answers must be in sentence form, not just a word or phrase. If you ask, "How are you today?" and the contestant answers, "I am fin*e*," then he's out. If he had said, "I'm all right," he could have stayed in the game. Try to ask questions which will be interesting or funny.

Anguish Languish

A game for fifth-grade or older children that will stimulate creativity and hilarity can be described by the title of the book from which it was taken, *Anguish Languish* by Howard L. Chace. The best way to get it started is to read the following aloud. Then hope that the class will take it from there. Keep *Little Red Riding Hood* in mind as you read aloud. It'll sound better.

> Ladle rat rotten hut tucker ladle basking fuller shirker cockles end woke threw the lodge dock florist tour groin murders hearse, ware she met a bag bed woof.

Show the story as you read it by projecting it on the overhead projector. Let the students try to finish it. You can supply the *mural*:

> Ladle gulls shudder stopper torque wet strainers.

How to Enjoy Indoor Recess with Your Class

It was a dismal winter afternoon, one in a long series of below-zero days. The third-graders had not been outdoors for gym or recess for two weeks.

Class was called to order at one o'clock, and we waited for the usual chatterers to settle down. But it seemed that everyone was talking, even the ones who were usually quiet and attentive. I said, "If you want to talk so much, why don't you vote for it when we decide what to do during indoor recess?"

There was immediate silence—surprise followed by scheming looks. There was no doubt what was coming. At two-fifteen, when we were putting on the board four suggestions for their 15-minute recess, Vicki's suggestion was *Talking. Seven-Up* and drawing were duly listed. As usual, David suggested that I read from *Charlotte's Web*.*

Before the vote, I commented that we might change the name from *Talking* to *Conversation,* and we discussed choosing interesting topics. Everyone saw that if they all talked at once no one would have anyone listening to him, so we agreed on the merits of listening, replying, and "keeping the ball rolling" (staying with one topic until everyone had had something to say and felt ready to go on to something else).

Conversation won the vote by a landslide. Everyone was excited as they anticipated the break.

At the signal, children scurried into groups. Some went to the corners. Two or three sat beneath each table. One large group later divided. There was much animated talk. The listening one couldn't be sure of.

---

* E. B. White, Evanston Ill., Harper 1952.

An Experience with a Child Who Had Nothing to Say

One pair wandered up to me and asked if they could play with flash cards. "I can't think of anything to talk about," one of them explained. I suggested that he use the same subjects he uses when he is supposed to be paying attention in class. We laughed over that, and then I mentioned some after-school plans that he had with his friend. They left for their corner, chatting away.

There were moans and groans when the time was up. Everyone agreed that *Conversation* was a wonderful indoor activity—a welcome change.

In our lesson after recess, most of the children were calm and steady. The need to communicate had been satisfied for a while.

Since that day, my pupils choose *Conversation* often. They were never told that they were practicing language arts!*

As this experience suggests, our *Conversation* game can be a worthwhile indoor recess activity, leading to increased self-control. Be sure to set the rules ahead of time. We agreed not to go into the closet, but pupils were allowed under tables. Children were to move to their conversation place without running and pushing. Loud shouting and silliness would be reason for stopping the game. The main prohibition was never to leave anyone alone, but to include everyone.

Don't worry about the noise level, as other classes are playing indoor games at this time too. Shut your door and join in the fun. Be ready to chat with anyone who comes up to you. Never spoil this opportunity by marking papers and missing it. You will find out about new baby sisters, puppies, romances, and all sorts of family secrets you'd rather *not* hear.

This activity can serve you as a chance to observe your group in social interaction. It will prove to be even more effective than a sociogram in sorting out the social misfits so you can help them.

If you don't happen to have anyone to talk to, or listen to, it's very enlightening to eavesdrop just a little. You may be amazed to hear a little group discussing a recent world crisis, or another under-the-table session swapping recipes. You won't be sorry you had this experience, just sorry that you had to cut it short because their time was up.

---

* Rosalind Minor Ashley, "Let Them Talk," *The Instructor,* Vol. LXXVII, Number 5, Jan., 1968, p. 33.

CHECKLIST

Plan a regular Current Events time, which will not only help pupils to speak better, but will give them something interesting to talk about.

Have maps and globes available, which will be looked at carefully while discussing things that are happening *now*.

Teach health when news items about diseases, cures, and new medical experiments are brought up.

Use accidents which are mentioned as a springboard for teaching safety.

Discuss the weather as a science activity.

Give attention to each news item brought in, even if it is not given orally.

Encourage children to read as much of the newspaper as they're able to understand, and to get news from radio and television.

Teach discussion skills by defining and practicing the roles of leader and participants.

Allow children to review books in many ways: book sharing, chalk talks, creative dramatics, and other methods.

Organize a classroom club to give speech opportunities to all, as well as practice in democratic living and assuming responsibility.

Use story games and word games to practice speech, and to have a good time.

Allow an occasional free conversation period, after you set rules.

Utilize a free period of talk to observe children who need social help.

3

How to Build Listening Skills

The world is full of people who only half-listen. You talk to them every day, and will surely agree that adults, as well as children, need better listening habits. It's too late for most older people, whose habits are firmly established, but the teacher can still train young children to really listen, not just half-hear. It's a skill to be taught and practiced—it won't come by itself—so to develop the listening potential of our young charges we must begin now. There are a few simple methods you can try, and they are such fun that you'll find that your pupils will consider this a favorite part of their day.

A WAY TO FOCUS ATTENTION—YOU COULD HEAR A PIN DROP

You've probably developed several excellent ways to call your class to attention. Perhaps you clap your hands and wait. Maybe you stand in front and quietly stare at them. Other teachers may ring a bell. Some use a whistle on the playground, and many wish that they could use it in the room. Whatever method works for you, let's assume that each child is settled in his seat, most are looking at you, and at least two-thirds are ready to listen. You may be shocked by this fraction and not believe it, but it is the best you can expect at first. There are a few key words which might get the non-listeners' full attention. They are *recess, gym,* and *lunch.* Don't try them now.

When you're ready to start work, the reluctant listeners will put some thought into what you're saying. Our task is to get their complete attention. How can you prevent this waste? Try this idea. It's best to save it for your first special listening lesson. Then use it as a regular device for the rest of them.

Hold up a pin. Tell your group that you're going to drop it, and you'd like to know who has heard the pin touch the floor. You may want to remind them of the old expression, "It was so quiet you could hear a pin drop." Have them raise their hands as a signal to you that they've heard the pin reach the floor. To add to the importance of the moment, place a "Please Do Not Disturb" sign on the outside of your door. It gives a note of drama to the occasion. By now everyone is straining to listen. Hold the pin high and wait a few moments. Some of them will get a bit nervous and scrape their chairs. This will start a rash of chair-scraping. Wait. Just stand there and look at them, pin held high. At this time the room will be quiet —really still. Drop the pin and watch for hands.

It's amazing that children who often miss what you've said in a normal voice, will hear the tiny tinkling sound of a metal pin hitting the floor. Those who missed it might be disappointed. Give them another chance this first time. Drop it again. What are you accomplishing with all of this apparent nonsense? You're focusing their attention, something necessary in order for them to listen well. The only time that this didn't work too well was when we had some noisy crickets chirping in the room. If you'd like to drop something that makes a slightly louder sound, try a paper clip.

Are They Ready to Listen?

Many people make the mistake before a lesson, a story, or a record, of beginning too soon, before their audience is completely ready to stop what they were doing before. It's essential that you watch for this when pupils are going to speak or entertain for other children. Remind them to wait a few minutes in order to have a polite audience. Some children cannot rush from one activity to another. They need a few minutes in between to tie up the loose ends in their minds. This will only be effective if you're looking at them as you wait. If you stop to talk to a child or read something, your waiting time will do no good, as they will probably begin to talk to each other, or start some work on their desks. It's also wise to clear the desks.

You might be concerned about the necessity of dropping a pin for every lesson. It's not only unnecessary—it would destroy its effect to do it too often. However, keep in mind the excellent results you can obtain. They are certainly worth a few extra minutes.

What, then, is the difference between dropping the pin and all the other methods we've mentioned? It is the active participation of the child. The learner, to learn well, must *do* something. He can have a mental experience and participate fully. When you combine it with a physical one; something to touch, something to turn, something to taste, something to try out, something special to listen for, it makes a bigger impression. You should try it at least once. You have nothing to lose but a pin!

When you don't want to use a pin, just waiting and looking straight at your group will accomplish a great deal. If you hold up something as a display piece, it will serve as a focus for attention. You can use any type of object suitable to the lesson, as listening training must pervade all subjects. A picture, globe, piece of scientific equipment, book, or even a piece of paper will serve.

BUILDING LISTENING SKILL

Every good teacher has been reading aloud and speaking aloud to her pupils for years. What has been missing? The children were listening, weren't they? Some were, in varying degrees. Yet you know that for every dreamer you could see, there were at least five woolgatherers who could fool the teacher completely as they sat there.

Of course, you still want to talk to your class and read to them. This is good listening practice, once they have been taught *how* to listen, but some training must come first.

Use Listening Skill Builders Regularly

There is an excellent series of Listening Skill Builders available, which gives systematic training in listening.* The stories in the program are graduated in difficulty, and are meant to sharpen the child's ability to listen for details and main ideas. Because a teacher considers this activity very important, the children will also, and no one will raise a hand or make a noise once a story has begun. Post your "Please Do Not Disturb" sign first. You start with the Student Record Books closed. Have the children get ready to listen for your

---

* S. R. A. Reading Laboratory, Science Research Associates, Inc., 259 E. Erie St., Chicago, Ill. 60611.

signal that you're about to begin. They will raise their hands to let you know if they've heard the pin. Get their attention, drop the pin, and smile at them to let them know you've seen their hand signals. Then they are to listen as hard as they are able. When you read your story, read it as carefully and clearly as you can. After the story is completed, have the class open their record books to a special page where the questions for the Listening Skill Builders are to be answered. They will then see a page with numbered multiple choice phrases which complete a sentence. The teacher reads the beginning of the sentence only once, so the pupils are forced to listen intently.

After the children make their choices in pencil, have them check their work very carefully, and then color in the answers with colored pencils. Any change after the colored pencils are used must be initialed by you. It is most effective to write the answers on the board or overhead projector, so that the children can mark the answers on their own. After the scoring, show them how they can enter their scores on Listening Progress Charts in their Student Record Books. These books have a reverse side which will be used for reading, so they do double duty. The Listening Skill Builder activity, including story, marking, and record-keeping, does not take long, but you will get better, more satisfying, results on this than on most other things the children do. Pupils receive immediate reinforcement, and they take great pride in doing well on it. It's wonderful how attentive pupils *can* be. You'll wish that there were more of this attention during the rest of the day.

What Should We Do When We Listen?

We should try to accomplish the following when we listen:

1. Relate what we know to the speaker's statements.
2. Try to figure out his purpose in speaking.
3. Draw conclusions, keeping in mind how reliable we feel his purposes and information are.

Fifth- and sixth-graders can analyze a tape recorded speech using these points. This can lead to an interesting study of propaganda and mob formation.

PLAY GAMES

There are also a few simple games to use to develop listening skills.

Practice Making Introductions

An activity which will teach a necessary social skill, as well as build listening ability, is the practicing of introductions. The reason so many adults have difficulty in making introductions and find it so embarrassing, is that they neglect to listen when the name is given. Then, when they must introduce this person to someone else, there is a horrifying blank instead of a name. The following game for elementary pupils can be simplified for younger children. In order to make it a really effective lesson, try to time it before an Open House, or some occasion when a child will have to introduce his parents and grandparents to you. Then the practice will become truly important to him. It can still be good fun if you remember that children love to pretend and love secrets. Give each one a secret name on a piece of paper. He is to show it to no one. You can get in on the enjoyment too. Pretend to be someone's little brother. The procedure will be for you to get the game started by being the first pupil's little brother. Go up to Pupil No. 1, read his secret name, and bring him up to Pupil No. 2. Introduce them, using their new names. Bring Pupil No. 1 up to Pupil No. 3 and introduce them, looking at each secret name as you do. After you have introduced No. 1 to No. 4, then leave him on his own to bring these three children up to each other member of the class. No. 1 will use secret names only for Nos. 2, 3, and 4. He will use the real names of all other classmates. The listening practice will come in when the first introductions are made.

Everyone will want a turn, so if you run out of time before each person has a chance to introduce three new names to his friends, keep a record of where you left off, so you can begin there the next time. Once the rest of the group sees how much trouble No. 1 is having remembering the new names of Nos. 2, 3, and 4, they will be warned to listen well when they have an opportunity to hear the secret names. You will be able to give them a few simple rules at this time, teaching them the courtesies of making introductions to older people.

Simon Says

Simon Says is an old favorite for people of all ages. This game involves listening carefully to directions. A leader gives orders and the group obeys them. A sample of the game follows:

"Simon says, touch your toes."

Everyone touches his toes.

"Simon says, wiggle your nose and touch your left ear."

The group obeys.

"Now wiggle your nose and touch your right ear."

The few who wiggled their noses and touched their right ears are out of the game. They must not follow the order unless it follows "Simon Says." If they follow a direct order without these two words, they're out. The orders may be anything possible for the group to do easily. The main idea is not to make it impossible for them to obey. It is to catch them when they're not listening well.

It's much more interesting for the pupils if you vary your listening skill-building lessons. For example, alternate a listening activity in which children listen for details and main ideas leading to better comprehension, with other lessons in which they listen for particular sounds or syllables.

Use Accent Cards

Some exercises which may be useful are described below. They will not always be used at specific grade levels. Need determines use.

A good third- or fourth-grade practice exercise for accented syllables is one in which each child uses a tagboard card with an accent mark on it. These must be prepared ahead of time, and collected after the lesson for future use. The teacher slowly reads a familiar word as the class listens. The word is slowly repeated. The second time, the child puts up his accent mark card as he hears the accented syllable. The primary accent is the only one used. This exercise encourages individual responses more than the practice of calling on individuals.*

Read Poetry Aloud for
Phonics Practice

You might enjoy trying a lesson in which you read aloud any poem. Choose a particular sound for the day. You can decide between simple vowel sounds or more difficult blends. You might want to begin with listening for the long *a* sound. You could use any approach you prefer, either having children raise hands when they hear

---

* Rosalind Ashley, "Linguistic Games and Fun Exercises," *Elementary English*, The National Council of Teachers of English, Vol. XLIV, No. 7, Nov., 1967, p. 765.

each sound, or having them write the words as they hear them. Hand raising seems more suitable for younger children, as they will have difficulty writing the words fast enough to keep up with you. If you decide to have them write words containing the special sound, it's a good idea to have the poem written out and projected by the overhead projector, so they can refer to it. To illustrate how this lesson would go, read the following poem aloud, listening for a long *a* sound.

SPRING

by Rosalind Ashley

1. The jonquils nod their golden heads
2. To buds unseen,
3. And whisper in their rocky beds,
4. "Awake—be green!"
5. The chill wind carries promises of balmy days.
6. "Awake!" the chill wind cries.
7. "Awake, buds—unfurl your eyes."
8. "Awake, arise!"
9. "Sun—glow your rays!"
10. And the world obeys.

As you *slowly* read the poem for your class or reading group, they will (or should) raise their hands when they hear the following words:

awake	— Line 4		awake	— " 8
days	— " 5		rays	— " 9
awake	— " 6		obeys	— " 10
awake	— " 7			

Many children will raise their hands at the word *their* in Line 1. This will give you an opportunity to teach the vowel *a* which is influenced by an *r*. It is not considered a long *a*, but has a mark like this: *â*.

Compose Your Own Skill Builders

You can compose your own listening skill-building lessons which pinpoint the specific phonic needs of your group. A sample exercise which teaches discrimination between the *wh* sound and the *w* sound follows.

Read it aloud and ask for raised hands when pupils hear the *wh* sounds. Read the paragraph again, and ask for pupils to raise their hands when they hear the *w* sound. You may wish to have them write the answers after this. Read the exercise aloud at least two more times, pronouncing it very distinctly.

> When was the wagon wheel with the whirring, whizzing noise wending its way west to Wheeling, West Virginia? Which wheel of the whirring, whizzing wagon wheels whizzes the worst? Why was the wide, white wagon loaded with wood, wheat, and watermelons?

As you can see, it doesn't have to make too much sense. In fact, the children like it better when it's a bit silly. It needn't be boring in order to accomplish your aim.

An important activity to precede and follow this listening lesson is one in which all of the pupils hold their hands to their lips and say "whizzing." Ask them if they feel their breath on their hands. If not, they must keep saying the word until they do. Try the word, "wagon." They will not feel any air on their hands. It's necessary to teach the proper pronunciation of *wh* and *w* before you begin, so the pupils will be very sure what they're listening for. They are also developing a habit of correct pronunciation.

Compose a little article related to some science or social studies unit you plan to teach. You will be using science ideas and facts at the same time you teach listening for details and main ideas.

Read the article aloud. Have answer choices written on a transparency on the overhead projector. After you finish reading, start immediately to ask the questions. The class will write capital letters identifying their answers. Circle the capital letters before the correct answers on the transparency, so the children can mark their work. Be sure to discuss the article and clear up any questions that they may have. Ask the people who got them all correct to raise their hands. Tell them that they've done well. You can also comment that those who missed one or two are making progress.

Any story or article which teaches something can be used. It is better to write one for a unit you have not covered yet. It's unavoidable that some children will give answers from what they already know, but you want them to concentrate on their listening as much as possible.

Sample Skill Builder

A sample article with questions follows:

INSECTS

There are a few things which set insects apart from other creatures. Try to examine an ant or a fly to see these things for yourselves.

Insects have six legs and a jointed body. In a fully-grown insect you'll find three pairs of legs. The name *insect* comes from a term that means *in sections,* or jointed.

An insect's jointed body has three sections. The front part is the head. Attached to the head are *antennae* or *feelers.* The middle section is called the *thorax.* The insect's six legs are attached to this. The back section, or *abdomen,* comes behind the thorax. The wings are attached to the abdomen, and often hide it.

There are many creatures that look like insects which are not true insects. You have an exact way of telling the difference. Count their legs. See if their bodies are divided into three sections.

If you find a buglike animal with eight legs, you may discover that it is a spider, mite, chigger, or tick. If the creature has 30 or more legs it's a centipede. The name might fool you into thinking it has 100 legs. Millipedes have 60 or more legs. This is enough to prove that they are not insects.

Spiders have two body sections, so this is another bit of evidence to show that they are not insects.

Most insects, at some time in their lives, develop wings. This is something else which sets them apart from other crawling animals.

QUESTIONS FOR TEACHER TO READ ALOUD

1. All insects have

2. All insects have

3. Most insects have

ANSWERS TO BE PROJECTED ON SCREEN

1. A. wings all their lives.
   B. six legs.
   C. four legs.

2. A. one body part.
   B. two body parts.
   C. three body parts.

3. A. wings at some time.
   B. feelers attached to their abdomens.

C. abdomens attached to their heads.

4. Spiders

4. (A.) have eight legs.
   B. have six legs.
   C. can fly.

5. The *main* differences between buglike creatures and insects are

5. A. insects can crawl and have two pairs of legs.
   B. insects can fly and have two body parts.
   (C.) insects have three body parts and six legs.

Listen to Music

You may wish to use music as a way of improving listening ability and teaching music concepts at the same time. Your music supervisor will be glad to help you with this if you need it. Use a record, or tape record a special musical selection using different kinds of notes and rests. Play it several times. Then ask the children to identify eighth notes, dotted half-notes, rests, and special rhythms as they listen again. Have them listen for one special thing at a time and raise their hands when they hear it. This will teach them a great deal about musical rhythm and also sharpen up their listening.

A delightful way to build listening skills for third- and fourth-graders through music and story is to use one of the many records available. An example is *Peter and the Wolf* by Prokofieff.* This particular record tells a story to beautiful music, as it teaches the sounds of many musical instruments.

The narrator tells the adventure, and the background music is played by the instrument which represents the character appearing or involved in the main action at this point in the story. The characters and the instruments that represent them are listed below:

Character	Musical Instrument
bird	flute
duck	oboe
cat	clarinet
grandfather	bassoon
wolf	three horns

* Centennial Symphony Orchestra, Radio Corporation of America, 33⅓ R.P.M. Camden, CAL-101, Side 1.

Peter   string quartet
the shooting of the hunters   kettle drums and base drum

The children will not only learn to recognize the sound of the respective instruments, but they will also remember the melody or theme given to each character. Added to the enjoyment and excitement of this wonderful story will be the thrill of recognizing each instrument for the respective characters. When two characters interact, their two instruments and themes are played in such a way that you can recognize each, and still enjoy their harmony.

In order to get the full listening benefit from this activity you will need to play the record several times, and then you should repeat it once in a while. The pupils will get to know grandfather's deep voice as it booms through the notes played by the bassoon, and Peter's theme will become very familiar. The children will shiver with excited anticipation when they hear the three horns signifying the dangerous wolf. This can become an experience deeply satisfying on two levels; educationally, and aesthetically.

Help Pupils Create a
Bulletin Board

This listening and music lesson can be extended to include research and art. It can result in a bulletin board which each child has shared in creating. Assign a character with its musical instrument from *Peter and the Wolf* to each child, or to committees. Have them do research in encyclopedias and music books to find out what each instrument assigned looks like. They are to draw sketches from the pictures in reference books. Later, pupils can color or paint the pictures, cut them out, and attach them to a bulletin board. To match the instrument, the child can create a picture of his own character, paint it, and cut it out. Give the class a rough idea of how tall or large each character should be to fit well with the other pictures. A committee can be assigned which will be responsible for making letters for the title. Choose a color for the title letters, which will be cut from colored construction paper. Obtain heavy yarn in a matching color, and have the pupils pin the yarn from the character to the musical instrument which represents the character. For example, the yarn will go from a picture of Peter to a picture of four violins grouped together. Show the children how to stretch the yarn so it is taut, pin it, and cut it to the correct length. Some of them can write the story of *Peter and the Wolf* in their own words. They will do a better job of it if they listen to the record before or after class, write the story, and then listen to the record again to fill in missing parts. They should copy it neatly, and attach it in the center of the bulletin board. If the characters with their matching instruments are circled around the bulletin board in an attractive manner, with the important characters near the center, this can be a very dramatic display. To add a touch of interest, have a few children draw and cut out musical notes in construction paper in the color chosen. Spread them around the bulletin board to inform viewers that this relates to music, in case they have never heard of the selection.

There are many other records available which teach the sounds of musical instruments, but none approach the drama and sheer delight of this exciting story.

Use Mood Music for Art

Perhaps you have tried this already, but if not, you will find this next activity very different from most classroom procedures. Choose any recording which projects a very definite and obvious mood. Let the children listen to it, to get a feeling from the music. Allow no interruptions as they listen. Then pass out art paper and have the class draw whatever they felt from the music. They may wish to draw an abstract design showing how the mood of the record affected them. Discuss how certain colors represent feelings. For instance, red, orange, and yellow are the warm, cheerful colors. If pupils would like to express a sad, gloomy mood they can use blue, purple, gray, or black. Now that they're ready to begin, have the children write their names on the back of their papers and start the record again. Allow no one to ask a question aloud to interrupt the mood. If someone raises a hand, signal him to come up to whisper to you. You may discover some records of your own that would be very suitable for inspiring a certain mood, or your school library may have something you can use. If you borrow a recording from a public library be very sure to listen to it and record even the slightest catch or scratch on it. Report this to the librarian before you sign it out. Otherwise, you probably will be charged for this damage later. A record which has been used successfully to create a mysterious, somber, scary mood is *A Night on Bare Mountain,* by Moussorgsky.* This might be a good activity for late October, just before Halloween. You will be happy with the intent listening and the creative results in art you'll obtain. To inspire a light, merry feeling which will result in a bright, gay design, or a scene from a story which has magic or happy adventures in it, you might wish to use *Sorcerer's Apprentice*, by Dukas, Band 1.* Another lighthearted piece is *Till Eulenspiegel's Merry Pranks*, by Strauss.†

Combining Listening with Note-Taking Instruction

An important listening skill that many teachers ignore is note-taking. It is closely related to finding the main idea in reading. If you're fortunate enough to have television receivers available, plan on combining instruction and practice in note-taking with the regular television viewing. Prepare lapboards from heavy cartons or cardboard. Place two rubber bands on each, to hold the paper. Remind pupils to take pencils with them if the set is out of your regular classroom. You should have a brief discussion before the program, in order to prepare the class for the vocabulary. Get them ready for efficient note-taking by emphasizing that they will not have time to write down everything they think is important. Demonstrate how to sort out the key words in a sentence by trying out a few. Read a paragraph for them and show them how you write only a word or two from each main idea. Let them know that this is not the time for complete sentences, and that a word here and there will remind them of an entire idea later. If they write too much it destroys the program for them, and they have no time to look at the screen or to think and react. You can vary this practice by reading a paragraph and having a volunteer write the main words on the board. Ask the class for their opinions on the words chosen. Be sure to allow time after the television program to use the notes they have taken. A good discussion should result from them. If television is not available, notes may be taken from lessons.

To Repeat or Not To Repeat

Many teachers have strong feelings on how to teach listening skills. A few have claimed that they will never repeat anything, no matter

---

* Warwick Symphony Orchestra, Radio Corp. of America, 33⅓ R.P.M. Camden, CAL-118, Side 1, Bands 1 and 2.

† Centennial Symphony Orchestra, Radio Corp. of America, 33⅓ R.P.M. Camden, CAL-101, Side 2.

what they're teaching. Even if it would work, which I doubt, most educators do not believe in this practice. If you will put yourself in the position of a child hearing something for the first time, perhaps uncertain of his ability to do the lesson, you will empathize with him and give him another opportunity to hear the directions if he needs to ask. You have probably needed to hear something repeated yourself, as do most people. There is nothing more likely to create a tense, unhappy child than the feeling that he cannot ask a question or have a second chance. It is an entirely different situation in a listening skill builder. Here the pupil understands the necessity for the teacher's refusal to repeat. This is a specific lesson for listening, and his other schoolwork will not suffer by his missing something. There are too many situations inherent in the school situation which cause tension, and there are too many disturbed children, without adding to their emotional burdens. When pupils must concentrate very hard to keep up or else miss something on a special listening lesson, the intensity is of a different kind; it is exciting, as in a game.

Let Them See It Too

If you will try to imagine how a child feels as he listens to new material, perhaps you will remember how it was when someone gave you directions or taught *you* something. The chances are that they said it too quickly. It was easy for *them*, because they knew it. Try to remember these experiences when you give directions to your group, or when you introduce something new or difficult. Say it slowly, repeat it, and make an effort to present it to at least one other sense, the visual, by writing your main points on the chalkboard or on the overhead projector. Listening is only one avenue to understanding, and we increase our effectiveness when we reinforce our speech with other methods. The very words *audiovisual equipment* remind us that seeing goes well with hearing, and we should use every method we can. Some children learn better visually. Remember that if a child misses what you've told him, it may be due to the fact that you said it too quickly. If you repeat it too quickly, he still won't get it. Make your life simpler and your pupils' work better by giving the children every chance to learn easily and happily, with no strain.

WHY DO YOU NEED TWO FOR A CONVERSATION?

Some talk sessions held between two people will not qualify as real conversations. In these cases, one person is busy talking about something of interest only to himself, and his partner is rehearsing what he will say as soon as he has an opportunity to break into the other person's talk.

Role-Playing

It might be fun to have two children pretend to have a talk like this. Try to show the class that each person in this demonstration is interested in himself alone, and does not hear a word said by the other one. Have one talk on the subject of something he cares about a great deal, and after the next person speaks on his own topic a while, have the first child go on just as though nothing was said. You've all heard talk like this.

Analysis—Is It a Conversation?

Ask the entire class to analyze this situation, and discuss *why* it is not a real conversation. Help them to reach these conclusions:

1. You must listen to what the other person says to you, instead of thinking about what you're going to say.
2. Your talk must be an answer to what you've just heard. If you haven't listened, you won't have anything intelligent to answer.
3. When you bring up a new topic, make sure it's interesting to someone else besides yourself.

Have two other pupils demonstrate a real conversation. They should both speak on the same subject, and the second person to speak must say something that follows what the first one has just said.

Praise all of the performers and comment that the first two had boring talk, but the second pair had an interesting conversation, a very good way to really get to know and like someone.

COMBINE LITERATURE, LISTENING, AND FRESH AIR

Children need interesting things to listen to, as well as specific training in how to get everything possible out of an experience. There are endless lists of records, tapes, filmstrips with matching records, and other listening materials. Any of these will make good listening practice.

Literature

If you tell a good story or read some fine literature, the children
will enjoy the experience and benefit from their previous training.
The book you read aloud should be one you like. *Charlotte's Web,*
or any of the *Pippi Longstocking* stories will be a treat for all concerned. The story chosen must fit the interests of the age level, but
not match their reading level too strictly, as children can understand
more difficult books than they can read on their own. Some pupils
love to obtain the book and read along with you silently as you read
aloud.

Story Records

With a busy curriculum there are few chances to spend the time
on story records, so choose them with care. You may have an indoor recess or a birthday party time which will provide your opportunity. Danny Kaye has made a fine one, called *Danny Kaye Tells
Six Stories From Faraway Places.** The humor, dramatic skill, and
background music make this worthwhile listening, even if it is on
regular school time.

Filmstrips with Matching Recordings

There are filmstrips available which are synchronized to records.
You get the filmstrip ready on the title frame. Have the record player
warmed up, and the record on. Start the record playing, and change
the filmstrip frames when the record gives you a sound signal. The
combined filmstrip-record learning experience is available in many
subjects, and is excellent listening practice.†

Outdoor Listening

The most fun of all for a teacher can be a day when it's too hot
to work in the classroom. Be prepared for this day when it comes.
If you are fortunate enough to have a playground with a few trees,
or a nearby park, be ready with a tiny campstool, wristwatch, and a

---

* Danny Kaye and Sylvia Fine, Arthur Shimkin Enterprises, 33⅓ R.P.M.
Golden Record, LP 62.

† SVE, Society for Visual Education, Inc., 1345 Diversey Parkway, Chicago, Ill.

big hat, plus the attitude that it's worth a little bother in order for you and your pupils to be comfortable. You've probably been trying to read something wonderful to the class in your spare time, and finding that you never have any spare time. When it's very humid, over 90°, and most other classes are just enduring the day—now is your chance. Send a note to your principal so that he'll know where you are. Tell the group that you're moving your class outdoors where they'll be cooler, and inform them of the behavior you will expect. Assign a few willing helpers to carry your stool, your hat, and your book, and line the children up to go outdoors in the cool shade. They will be so delighted that they will be an excellent audience. You will get an opportunity to read aloud something you've been putting off due to lack of time, the children will have an enjoyable listening experience, and a potentially wasted hour will become valuable. Lessons and discussions can also be done very well in the fresh air. You'll do it often, and once you see how happy and well-behaved a class can be while listening to a story outdoors, you won't even need the excuse of a hot day.

CHECKLIST

Get your pupils' full attention (as much as possible) before you begin anything.

Try dropping a pin as a special means of focusing pupils' attention for regular listening skill-building lessons.

Try something special to listen for as a way to improve listening.

Treat the listening sessions as important, and your class will too.

Analyze tape recorded speeches, listening for motives and reliability, before studying propaganda and mob formation.

Teach social graces as well as listening by having role-playing with introductions.

Play *Simon Says* for listening practice and fun.

Use tagboard cards for a listening exercise teaching accented syllables.

Read poetry aloud for listening training in hearing special vowels, consonants, or blends.

Devise listening exercises for special sounds to meet individual or group needs.

Write your own listening lessons based on future science or social studies units.

Listen to records or tapes for musical identification of notes, rests, and special rhythms.

Create a listening lesson and bulletin board from the recording of *Peter and the Wolf*.

Use recordings to project a particular mood, and inspire drawings or paintings in this way.

Provide instruction and practice in note-taking from oral classroom and television lessons.

Remember, as you teach, that it is not always possible or easy to remember many details when you hear them at once, or if they are said to you quickly.

Utilize two senses by showing things to pupils as they listen.

Teach the art of conversation by role-playing experiences, showing the correct way, as well as giving a horrible example of how *not* to talk to someone.

Use every resource available to provide listening practice that is rich in information and enjoyment.

Conduct outdoors classes whenever possible, reading stories, or having lessons and discussions.

4

Developing Practical Uses
for Creative Dramatics

The most natural thing for children to do is to act or pretend. They role-play for fun all the time while they play. A very logical question for you to ask then, is why give them school time for something they're going to do anyway? There are several reasons. They need some guidance in dramatics, voice projection, and in creating scenes in sequence from a basic idea or story. The social values coming from planning, creating, and rehearsing together are a result of an organized, supervised experience. Once there is adequate pupil leadership and a planned continuous series of scenes, and once some guidelines and limits are drawn, the children can be encouraged to rehearse at each other's homes, in order to save classroom time. This relates to the creative dramatics which the typical classroom teacher would plan as language arts and social learning. We are not, of course, describing the creative dramatics taught by a specialist, leading to an all-school performance. In fact, the very informality and relaxed attitude toward the actual stage performance is what makes this so worthwhile.

Some teachers will agree that creative dramatics is valuable, but they claim they have no time for it. Others may wish to teach it, but avoid it because they have had no formal training, or do not know exactly what it is. Creative dramatics is informal and grows spontaneously. It includes role playing, dramatic play, dramatization and pantomiming. In the kindergarten and primary grades children have experiences in unrehearsed playmaking, as they dramatize familiar stories and prepare puppet shows. They are able to enter into their characterizations realistically.

In the intermediate grades, children are increasingly self-conscious, and they select more structured plays with definite plots. It is very important to help them to maintain the freedom, realism, and enjoyment of creative dramatics developed earlier, and to progress in the ability to express emotion through speech and pantomime.

Third-graders enjoy dramatizing stories with flannel boards in connection with Individualized Reading, and some team up to act out short scenes from their books.

Specific ways of using creative dramatics for an assembly will be described in this chapter, with special attention given to avoiding the dangers of stagefright and tension that result from giving the idea of an audience too much importance. The way to minimize the disturbance caused by a clown, or the tension caused by memorization of scripts, will be discussed. Reasons are given why we need to find time for dramatics, no matter how busy we are.

How to Team Creative Dramatics and Individualized Reading

Since one of the many advantages of Individualized Reading is the opportunity it gives for teacher and pupil to plan follow-up activities after the completion of the individual's book, we will agree that the dramatic scene should be optional for those who need and desire it. Many shy children who need this creative outlet will try it once they've been inspired by other pupils' enjoyment of it; but it should not be forced. When a child wishes to present a scene, the first step is to find other children who have read the same book. In case no one has read it yet, select one or two volunteers to read it, perferably fast readers. When the children are ready, meet with them to help them choose the scene they think would appeal most to the class. Once this is decided, suggest that they list the main events in this scene in the order in which they happened. After this, let them alone for a while to plan it. It will seem very disorganized at first, but their enjoyment will lead to many rehearsals, polishing it each time.

When they are ready to show it to you, check to see whether they cover the listed main events in the scene. Another thing to watch for is whether the flavor of the book is coming through to the audience. Remind them not to make it too long. Once this has been done, give them complete freedom to compose their own dialog and action. Provide encouragement, as well as simple props if they are needed. Too many rehearsals may destroy the children's spontaneity, so allow them to present their scene as soon as they say they're ready. Schedule the scene for one afternoon just before school is dismissed. The cast should have the book's title and author written clearly on the board, so that those who would like to read the book can copy them down.

IT'S YOUR TURN TO PLAN AN ASSSEMBLY

It would be much better for your children to present their creative dramatics plays for small audiences; for example, for two or three other classes in their own grade level. The main reason for this is to maintain the relaxed freedom of the creative play given for their own pleasure and growth, which they wish to share.

However, if an all-school assembly program is your responsibility, consider combining music with the choral reading of poetry. If you still wish to give a dramatic presentation, plan ahead by having your children prepare two separate plays creatively, thus giving each child a turn. These plays can be practiced and presented early in the year for just their own classmates. Then, when the assembly program is near, the children can practice them a few times and present the plays as originally given, feeling that they are doing something familiar. This is suitable for children *over* ten.

Preparation

To help elementary level children to characterize, the teacher should introduce the subject by giving them an example of pantomime. It might be a shy young girl about to enter a room where there is a party. The girl is nervous, and she keeps fixing her hair and clothing. She looks many times in the mirror, and is constantly clearing her throat. The class can try to guess who she is, how she feels, and where she is.

Ask the class to observe people and try to imagine what they're feeling. Explain pantomime to them and let them try to do it, first in some simple action as themselves, then as other characters. Let them try out the following:

1. A man tiptoeing into his home very quietly, and then hearing the door creaking.

2. A comedian telling a joke, and realizing that nobody is laughing at it.
3. A girl trying to eat something she doesn't like at a dinner party, because she wants to be polite.

Encourage all children whether they do well or not, but special praise for those who have planned well will raise the value of the experience and the quality of their work.

Next they can try improvisations with dialogue between two or more characters. This activity is especially interesting if the participating children think of their own climax.

Story Selection

A group of imaginative, uninhibited children can enjoy composing their own plot with adult guidance, showing the teacher much about their thinking. However, dramatizing a well-written story tends to widen their horizons.

Cast Selection

The fairest way is to select the cast from those children who volunteer. Choose a few pupils with ability to carry the scene so that it will get a good start and thus give the group a feeling of success. In the middle of the period give turns to those who have had none. Try to give each child a chance to choose the part he wishes to play, continuing the next day if time runs out.

"Action"

Allow older children to play a scene through to the end without interruption. In cases where the cast is floundering—and this is usually the result of insufficient planning—you should stop and talk it over before trying again. Even familiar stories should be read carefully more than once. Talk over what happens and who the characters are, and then decide on a starting point. First, everyone must get to know the characters, and then plan the action, leaving out less important episodes. If necessary, a narrator can make the transitions. Discuss the setting, and start with a bit of action to get the feel of the characters. A whole group often tries some one character at the same time.

Use music to set the mood. Some children who are self-conscious in talking can let go when carried along by the music, and all have freer bodily expression with music. Then begin at the first part of the story and play a small section, ending with an entrance or an exit. Twenty children make an ideal group, so all can have enough turns. Each day the main ideas will emerge clothed in new language. Words or gestures are not memorized—only the skeleton of the story. The words must be fluid, as in normal conversation, and not become set in a mold.

SUGGESTED ACTIVITIES—ROLE PLAYING

Children play familiar characters, using known situations of home and school, as well as current happenings. Social studies, literature, or science materials can be integrated into an organized culminating dramatic activity as the conclusion of a unit of study. One third-grade teacher conducted a grocery store for about three weeks for the main purpose of giving practice in column addition. The children got an opportunity for role-playing as grocer, helper, or customer.

One variation of role-playing is to ask volunteers to present a given situation in pantomime, and have the class try to guess what it is. Some examples are given below:

You are a little boy and you're trying to turn on the television set, but you can't reach it. You keep looking at the clock and at the television guide, because it is time for your favorite program.

You see a dollar through an open grating in the street, but you can't reach it no matter how hard you try.

Of course, you'll have to tell the group what each scene was if they don't guess it.

Children in kindergarten, first, and second grade can role-play as well as older pupils, if you give them something familiar to do.

A five-or six-year old child is so much more uninhibited than other pupils that role-playing can be extremely useful in helping him to express his feelings. Use familiar stories, or situations in which happiness, fear, excitement, or fatigue can be shown. Discuss the various clues that people give us to show how they feel—the way they look and walk, and their nervous mannerisms. Use stories that are incomplete. Kindergarten and first-grade children can act out these stories, supplying their own endings. The class can have some good discussions as to whether the characters worked out their problems in thinking or non-thinking ways. By putting themselves in the role of the characters, pupils may get additional insight into methods they could use to solve their own problems. An example of an unfinished story follows.

Too Little

Billy was the smallest boy in the neighborhood. He was seven years old, but he just didn't seem to grow up like the other kids. Bobby in the next block, who was a half-year younger than Billy, was six whole inches taller.

One bright Saturday morning, Billy was sitting on the front porch wishing the children would finish breakfast and come out. He'd been waiting all week for this day because the neighborhood children planned to make a tree house in the woods.

Finally the twins, who were older and knew how to build things, walked by and waited on Billy's porch for Sam and Jim, who lived next to Billy. When all the boys were there, they started for the woods, carrying odd boards, hammers, saws, and nails.

They decided their house should be in a tree near the street so they could watch the people and cars passing by without anyone knowing they were there.

One by one they put the boards up and nailed them firmly in place. Billy kept asking if there was a job for him to do because everyone kept forgetting that he was there. They were all hammering and sawing, which were things that Billy had never done.

"I know, I can fix the roof out of leaves," suggested Billy.

The kids turned and looked at him, and Bobby said, "Oh, no, you can't; you're too little."

To the Teacher

After the children have role-played an ending, let them discuss why they think the story might have ended in the way they imagined. Encourage the children to think of other possible endings.

Other areas that have role-playing possibilities include:

1. Adjusting to larger groups;
2. Sharing the teacher with other children;
3. Sharing toys and materials;
4. Taking turns and waiting;
5. Seeing that the same thing is often done in different ways by different people;

6. Relating one's self emotionally to others outside of the family group.*

Role-playing may also be used in the battle against prejudice. Children of any age can experience what it feels like to be excluded if you carefully plan to discriminate against certain groups by turn. For example, you may choose blue-eyed blondes one day, or children with black hair on another occasion. On the day that they are to be excluded because of the way they look, no one will play with them, they will be left out of certain activities, and they will be made to feel very different and alone. If each child gets a turn for this activity he will be able to empathize with those who spend their lives this way.

CAN WE PREVENT STAGE FRIGHT?

We can never prevent, nor do we wish to, the exhilaration and excitement of the moments before any stage performance begins. What we must avoid is the paralyzing terror that causes children to freeze up, stammer, and avoid the stage from then on. We can prevent this traumatic fright by emphasizing the performers instead of the performance. The experience of dramatizing means more than the dramatic production, although the aim is always to entertain well if you can. To achieve this, use expression of ideas, referral to the book or story, enjoyable rehearsals with freedom to change dialogue constantly, and absolutely no planning of an audience. Once the children are happy with their play they'll beg to share it with others. Only then do you plan on whom to invite. If you keep the audience very young and very small the experience, not the play, will be "the thing." It is a good idea to allow parents of the performers to come to all plays if they wish, but do not specifically invite them. If they do come, let them know that this is just a learning experience, one of many, and that they are not coming to see a major production, with its unfortunate pressures on children. For children over ten, it will not be harmful to gradually increase the size and importance of their audience.

---

* Ralph H. Ojemann, Katherine Chownining, Alice S. Hawkins, *A Teaching Program in Human Behavior and Mental Health, Handbook for Kindergarten and First Grade Teachers*, (Cleveland, Ohio: The Educational Research Council of America, 1961). pp. 22, 137, 139, 140. Reprinted by permission of The Educational Research Council of America.

WHY IS THE AUDIENCE UNIMPORTANT?

The audience and the future performance should be of secondary importance for all informal drama. The emphasis must be placed on the experience and action of the present. Otherwise, the play will become merely a series of rehearsals directed by the teacher. For the children to be creating, they must be submerging themselves in the mood of the story and have no awareness of an audience. The goals are self-expression, confidence, and development of understanding of others.

WHAT TO DO WITH THE CLOWN

Clowning, overplaying, or getting out of character in order to make others laugh can spoil the mood of the scene, and, after one warning, it will have to be stopped in order to replace the clown. There will be no need for further action, as he has probably learned his lesson by being out of the play. To prevent this, it will be useful to explain that dramatics has rules, just like any game or sport. In order to have a good play from which everyone can enjoy dramatics and learn, each person must stay in character and not try to spoil the scene.

FOLLOW-UP DISCUSSION

Encourage all discussion to be impersonal and positive. Look for ways to improve characterization, using names of characters rather than of individuals. Ask for good points first, being liberal with praise and encouragement. When criticism comes, it should be full of suggestions for enriching the production, rather than destructive to the feelings of the performers.

SPEECH IMPROVEMENT

An incident that occurred in a creative drama class offers convincing proof of the wisdom of making concentrated efforts on speech improvement only when the occasion arises. Anne, aged ten, had a nasal, whiny voice, and a careless habit of dropping her *ing's*. She had listened politely to the leader's frequent hints about correcting the fault, but made no apparent effort in that direction. One day she was playing the part of a queen in the improvisation of a fairy tale. During the evaluation period at the end of the scene, her colleagues frankly expressed their opinions of her interpretation.

"Anne walked just like a queen," said one, "but when she sent the elf to get her cobweb shawl she sounded like a little girl with a tiny, squeaky voice."

"Yes," said another, "I thought a queen's voice ought to be soft and silvery, like music."

"And a queen would have said whole words, not pieces of ones, so all her subjects could hear her when she sat on the throne and made speeches," a third child remarked. "Anne would be more like Queen Rosamond if she would say her words like that!"

The leader stepped into the situation at once, eager to avail himself of this opportunity. "What do you think about these suggestions, Anne? Don't you agree with Billy and Jean and Tom that your queen didn't have a very soft and silvery voice, and that her subjects would have found her speeches pretty hard to listen to?"

"Yes," Anne responded sadly. "You know, I wish I did have a queen's voice, 'cause then I could play her more real . . . but . . . I don't know how to make a queen's voice."

This was the very chance for which the leader had been waiting so patiently. The child had actually expressed a desire to improve her voice because she wanted, above all else, to be able to "play the queen more real." The next 15 minutes were spent profitably explaining the technicalities of speech mechanism in a simple and delightful way. By using analogies familiar to children, likening the resonance chambers to the sound box in a violin or cello, the vocal cords to their strings, and other such comparisons, the subject of voice and speech reproduction was given attention.

Any leader who wants to improve the speech of his group should watch for such an opening and make immediate use of it when it appears. He will set no regular times for drills, but space them appropriately throughout the whole season.*

The tape recorder can be especially helpful in helping pupils to speak better. Tape record their rehearsals and play them back. This will allow children to evaluate themselves. Once they feel a need for speech improvement you can really help them. If you have the services of a speech therapist, listening to the tape recording will help you to make referrals and correct mild handicaps.

---

* Isabel B. Burger, *Creative Play Acting*, Second Edition, (New York: The Ronald Press Co., 1966), pp. 62-63. Reproduced by permission of The Ronald Press Co.

YOU CAN'T FORGET YOUR LINES WHEN
YOU DON'T KNOW THEM

We often ask ourselves, "What is creativity, and how will we recognize it?" In the early grades it is much more important to give each child an opportunity to express his creativity than for the teacher to identify it. Nearly all young children are able to play creatively, and this ability can transfer to creative dramatics if we don't make the children self-conscious. The memorizing of a part channels concentration on learning of lines, and there is such fear of forgetting that most of a child's natural charm and spontaneity is lost, as well as his enjoyment of the experience. Avoid memorizing of plays, as it tends to inhibit children and make them self-conscious before an audience.

In creative dramatics, children create their own dialogue to tell their story, changing it at will. While the dialogue does tend to stay pretty much the same due to many rehearsals, the exact wording differs and is spontaneous, rather than memorized. This enables children to speak freely without the blocking caused by forgetting the first line. Since they know what they're talking about they'll easily find some words to say it. If they interrupt each other a bit, it is even more like natural speech. Memorization of lines may be good memory training, but it causes stiff, stilted dialogue, and the horrible fear of forgetting.

WE HAVE NO TIME FOR DRAMATICS—
REBUTTAL

You may have a special teacher for creative dramatics. If so, perhaps you will need to substitute for her at times. If the responsibility is all yours, never begrudge the time spent on creative dramatics. By its nature it is relaxing and offers a break which can be refreshing. If you are pressed for time, you may wish to integrate it with other subjects.

No school authority or parent expects or wants you to delve into the psyches of your pupils in order to diagnose latent mental illness. In fact, it is wise to have children play the part of others, as psychodrama is best left to those specially trained for it. However, the very open nature of creative dramatics makes it an excellent outlet for the repressed emotions of children. One teacher had her group play the roles of teacher and pupils, helping them to release their feelings and hostilities.* This alone would give dramatics great value, but it can also serve as a slight clue to disturbance. Reinforced by daily classroom observation, creative dramatics can help you to identify emotionally disturbed children who should be referred for testing by school psychologists. Any extreme of behavior can be a sign. This is another example of the worth of creative dramatics. In any case, it's a joyful group activity needed by children, leading to rapport with the teacher and within the peer group.

---

* Renata Morse, Milwaukee, Wisconsin.

CHECKLIST

Children need guidance in dramatics, voice projection, and in creating dramatic scenes in sequence from an idea or story.

Creative dramatics includes role-playing, dramatic play, pantomiming, and dramatization.

Children will enjoy dramatics as an optional follow-up activity for individualized reading, and will act out scenes from books.

Young children benefit from dramatics for its own sake, or for *casual* grade-level performances, with no emphasis on the audience.

Children over ten can give dramatic performances for school assemblies if they are plays practiced and presented earlier in the year, with importance given to the experience, and not to the perfection of the performance.

Pantomime is an excellent beginning for creative dramatics.

Improvisations with dialogue between two characters can follow.

When selecting one scene from a story, look for one which shows something about the plot or the main characters.

Plan carefully by having each actor thoroughly familiar with the story, all of the characters, and the setting.

Take enough time to discuss the story, plan together on the unimportant episodes which will be cut, and allow all of the players to try out each character.

Use role-playing for kindergarten and first-grade pupils too, having them dramatize incomplete stories.

Stagefright should, if possible, be prevented, but not the exhileration of performing well before a group.

Enjoyable, relaxed rehearsals, with no planning for an audience at first, can prevent the terror of performing.

Replace any actor who cannot follow the rules of the group, after sufficient warning. You can prevent this by discussing group goals at the start.

Allow follow-up discussions that are positive and impersonal, but discourage any criticism that will be destructive to a performer's feelings.

Make efforts at speech improvement only when the occasion arises and the child himself sees and feels the need for it.

Avoid all memorization for performances, as it inhibits children, makes them self-conscious and nervous, and deadens all creativity.

Try to make time for dramatics, as it is a fine outlet for feelings.

5

Games and Exercises
That Build Knowledge

Many teachers are guilty of calling nearly every lesson and exercise a game. Anyone would certainly approve of making the class *feel* that they're playing games, but we all know the difference between daily work and games, so it's a good idea not to call an exercise a game unless there is some element of fun or surprise in it. We fool no one, least of all our very perceptive pupils.

With this in mind, the following will include some real language games and some exercises that may be very enjoyable, but that should not be anticipated by pupils as a game. We must be heedful of a possible letdown when they say to themselves, "This is just work!"

It's Your Deal—
Switch Is Wild

One game that is suitable for third or fourth grade is called *Switch*. It is a card game designed to give practice on *word families*. Plan on groups of four or five. In each group choose someone who needs the honor of being the dealer. Some need it in order to achieve concentration in a group effort. Others may require it as a boost to self-confidence. You will need about forty 3x5 word cards in each set. The words listed below are just examples. You may change and add, according to your grade and needs:

bat	bad	cap	bag	ham	night	taught	can
cat	dad	lap	nag	jam	right	bought	fan
fat	had	map	rag	yam	sight	caught	man
hat	lad	nap	tag	ram	tight	fought	pan
mat	mad	tap	wag	tam	light	ought	tan

Each set contains four cards with the word *switch*. The dealer deals five cards to each child. The one on the dealer's left begins by putting down a card and naming it. Going clockwise, they take turns. The next player puts down a card that either rhymes with or begins with the same letter as the card laid down, saying it out loud. If a player has neither kind, he draws from a pack of extra cards until he can match the card laid down before or till he has drawn three. If he has a *switch* card he may name any word that rhymes or begins with the same letter. This named word is then played upon by the next player. The first one out of cards is the winner.

If the pack of extra cards is gone before there is a winner, the pupils play out matching cards until the pack is needed. Then the child with the fewest cards is the winner. If played as a lesson or indoor recess activity, plan ahead for each group to put their set of cards away and to read quietly while waiting for the other groups to end their games. It may also be used by a few children before or after school.

Other Games

An excellent series of language games which are good for small group remedial phonics work is called "Phonic Rummy."* Different sets in the series give practice in identifying and matching vowel sounds. Color is used for the vowel letters to be matched. These card games contain simple instructions, and children enjoy playing on their own once you get them started.

WHAT IS THE TEST-PATTERN METHOD?

In case this is a new term for you, it means testing a known word class in a slot in a sentence to see if it fits the word pattern. You try it out orally to listen to the pattern. Does it sound like the word order of normal English? You could say, "The *rallopash trimmed* up his *flibbles*." The noun *horse,* for example, does not fit in place of *trimmed*. This word slot needs a term that tells of something *done* to his *flibbles*. Common sense of what sounds correct, plus the test-pattern approach, will help your pupils to identify unknown words by their location in the sentence, their endings, and what they do

* Kenworthy Educational Service, Inc., Buffalo 1, New York.

to the words following them. Show the children that understanding of the word classes will lead to better sentences.

Some very fine material on the order of English and word form-classes can be found in *Discovering Your Language*, by Neil Postman, Harold Morine, and Greta Morine.*

> When words from the English language are not in an acceptable order, the speaker cannot be understood by his listeners. Furthermore, English-speaking people may use the same words in two different acceptable orders and thereby express entirely different meanings. The order of English words is of basic importance. The words listed below are arranged in different orders:
>
> 1. girls helped mother the their
> 2. mother their girls helped the
> 3. the girls helped their mother
> 4. the mother helped girls their
> 5. the mother their helped girls
> 6. their mother helped the girls
> 7. their helped the mother girls
>
> There are many more possible arrangements that could be made of the words. Of the seven sentences above, only two have meaning for us. The two sentences that have meaning are rather strange. Simply by rearranging the words the speaker can completely change the meaning of what he is saying. In the first meaningful sentence (No. 3), the girls are helping and the mother is the one being helped. In the second sentence (No. 6), their relationships are reversed. It is, therefore, important in English that the order of the words be watched carefully or else you may say the opposite of what you wish to say.
>
> For words to work, as language, they must have an order, or a *pattern*. The following exercises will help pupils to make some discoveries about word groupings and how these groups of words patterns in our language:
>
> Place each of the words given below in the blank spaces found in Sentences 1 and 2. Make a list of those words that pattern in Sentence 1 and a list of those words that pattern in Sentence 2.
>
> 1. The _____ runs.   2. The boys _____.

race	man	girl		climb	player	grow
dog	swim	laugh		horse	car	deer
	crawl	elephant		breathe	hide	

---

* (New York: Holt, Rinehart and Winston, Inc., 1963), pp. 38-50.

3. Read each sentence below carefully. Tell whether each
   blank should be filled with a word which would fit into List
   1 or List 2.
   a. _____ the car.
   b. _____ a new hat.
   c. Get the _____.
   d. Airplanes _____.
   e. Cook the _____.
   f. Go over the _____.
   g. This _____ is cold.
   h. I am a _____.

Can you make any statements about the two lists of words
you have developed to show how they differ?

The main difference between them seems to be that the words in
one list cannot take the place of the words in the other list. All words
that pattern alike belong to the same word group.

Although the above lessons are presented in a book for the junior
high level, they seem suitable for earlier use.

THE GROBE WAS BLICKING THE BOMTERS—
FIND THE NOUNS AND VERB

THE "SECRET MESSAGE" TRANSPARENCY SERIES

If you'd like to liven up your textbook grammar lessons, try preparing a set of simple transparencies for the overhead projector or
make a few posters using the following samples. We could call the
series "Secret Messages." These are very basic supplementary lessons,
and they may be started in the third grade, or used for fun and review
in the fourth and fifth grades. This series will give practice in identifying nouns, determiners, verbs, adjectives, and adverbs in simple
sentences. All of these word classes are also used in nonsense sentences. Write the typewritten or pencil originals in large capital letters
on any paper. A primary typewriter has large print, and is excellent
for preparing visuals. To make transparencies, use the special infra-
red machine which is usually available in your school office or Educational Services Center.* Special transparency material is usually
available nearby. No. 127 or No. 133 will work well. Place the plastic

---
* Visual Products Division, 3 M Company, 2501 Hudson Rd., St. Paul, Minn.,
55119.

on top of your prepared paper copy, with the notched part in the upper right corner. Feed them both through the machine together, after setting it for the correct color, according to the directions. Colored No. 129 transparencies are often available too.

Plan your supplementary series as a unit to teach word classes following regular textbook lessons, and make them up all at the same time. Use each transparency separately, as a culminating lesson before you go on to a new word class.

Some exercises build on the signalling devices, or clues, in structural grammar and use the idea of decoding a secret message. A clue is something in the words themselves, usually a suffix. Have the pupils identify the word class of the nonsense words.

A suggested color code follows. Be consistent and try to write the words later shown in italics in the color you have chosen:

nouns—red   adjectives—green
determiners—orange   adverbs—purple
verbs—blue

Nouns

First introduce nouns in your textbook, assign and mark some practice exercises, review, have an oral quiz, and then use your transparency with the secret message. If you try to use this series just for lesson work, it will not do the job, but it will serve well as an effective review and fun-filled activity to keep your grammar lessons from getting monotonous. Do not feel that you cannot use supplementary material from structural linguistics with textbook lessons that teach transformational grammar. There is no conflict. The following transparency material on nouns has been effectively used as a bulletin board lesson and display. If possible, set off in red the nouns and the words in italics.

SECRET MESSAGE

THE *BLOOBS* SAW THE *TOBES*.

TRY ANY OF THESE *NOUNS* IN PLACE OF THE SECRET *WORDS*.

| DEN | ZEBRAS | COBRAS | UNCLES | LEADERS | AUNTS | RAT |
| CAT | ZOO | MAN | SCOUTS | HORSES | BATS | COT |

DO YOU GET THE *MESSAGE*?

CLUES TO *NOUNS*:
THE AND *A* ARE *DETERMINERS* OR *NOUN MARKERS*.
NOUNS MAY HAVE THESE *ENDINGS*: *S, ES, S'*, AND *'S*.
NOUNS CAN BE REPLACED IN A *SENTENCE* BY OTHER
SIMILAR *WORDS*.

Revelation Method

You can get the most from your overhead projector lesson in the following way. Show the transparency, using the revelation method. This is a simple, effective means of making the best presentation. It keeps the class from getting ahead of the point you're making by covering everything but what you're using. You reveal the title and first line, keeping the rest covered with a sheet of paper, or any opaque material placed on the stage of the projector. The rest of the visual is kept covered until you are ready to reveal it. After this, you may wish to uncover the next two lines; all you have to do is move the paper down. When you get so near the bottom that your covering paper starts to slip off, you can keep it there by putting an eraser on it.

After you show the secret message, read it aloud. Then try out the suggested nouns in the slots containing nonsense words. Some will make sense and some will not, depending upon their meaning. Ask the class for their ideas on decoding the secret message. Then reveal the visual's clues to nouns, and discuss them in relation to the secret message nouns you've chosen.

Immediately after your first Secret Message on nouns, it would be effective to post the above Secret Message lesson as a bulletin board, with the nouns written on cards easily available in a box for the children to substitute in place of the nonsense words. You can use half of a hosiery box stapled to the bulletin board. As it will sag on the front side, punch holes in this side of the box, and tie colored yarn through these holes, stapling the other end of the yarn to the wall. It looks very dramatic to use red yarn to match the red noun letters. A sketch of the card box is shown in Figure 5-1.

Review the clues to nouns, and allow children to actually use the cards as an activity. In your earlier lessons they will have discussed the reasons why some of the listed nouns do not end in *s, es, s'*, and *'s*. They should also understand at this point how you can get these endings, and the reasons for them.

The only real change you need to make on the above material in order to make it a good poster display, is to add the word *cards* after

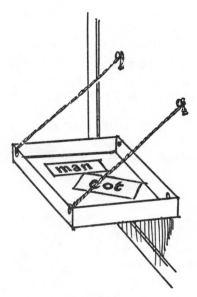

Figure 5-1.

noun so that the second sentence would read, "Try any of these *noun cards* in place of the secret *words*." The nouns would be written in red on separate tagboard cards, rather than be listed on the poster. The use of color is important. Red question marks near the title will add a bit of interest. If you begin with nouns color-coded in red, and if you are consistent throughout the year, this can become another device to help children identify and remember nouns.

In another lesson you can try these sentences:

Two *blinks* were caught.
The *blinks' faces* were very red.
Let's buy some *greekers*.

These nonsense words will become familiar as nouns because of their distinctive noun endings, *s* and *s'*.

The words which always point to or lead to nouns have been called noun markers after their function. It is best to use the correct word right away and call them determiners. Your next Secret Message gives practice in these. Try to write the determiners and words in italics in orange.

Determiners

SECRET MESSAGE

OBBLIP BOY IS COMING HERE.
THERE ARE *ZAMWICK* GIRLS.
FEED *CLABJOP* CAT *HIS* DINNER.

TRY ANY OF *THESE DETERMINERS* IN PLACE OF *THE*
SECRET WORDS:
THIS   THE   A   THAT   THOSE

DO YOU GET *THE* MESSAGES?

CLUES TO *DETERMINERS*:
DETERMINERS COME BEFORE NOUNS.
A DETERMINER ALWAYS HAS *A* NOUN FOLLOWING IT.
NOUNS ARE OFTEN USED WITHOUT *DETERMINERS*.
DETERMINERS MAY BE REPLACED IN *A* SENTENCE BY
WORDS THAT ACT *THE* SAME.

Verbs

Go on to verbs next. Repeat the same procedure: textbook lessons,
practice exercises, checking, review, oral quiz; and finish with the
Secret Message transparency lesson using verbs, which follows. Try
to write the verbs and words in italics in blue.

SECRET MESSAGES

THE ANIMAL *ROOLED* AND *RABBERED*.
THEN IT *RURPED*.
FOR ALL I *KNOW*, IT'S *RURPING* STILL.

TRY ANY OF THESE *VERBS* IN PLACE OF THE SECRET
WORDS.

CLIMBING	CLIMBED	CRAWLING	GROWLING
TALKING	GROWLED	WALKED	CRAWLED
	TALKED		

DO YOU *GET* THE MESSAGES?

CLUES TO *VERBS*:
VERBS FOLLOW THE SUBJECT IN THE SENTENCE.
VERBS ARE USED IN THE PREDICATE.

VERBS MAY *CONTAIN* THESE ENDINGS: *ED, ING.*
VERBS MAY *FOLLOW* WORDS LIKE: *WAS, WERE, HAVE,*
AND *HAD.*
VERBS MAY *BE REPLACED* IN A SENTENCE BY OTHER
WORDS THAT *ACT* THE SAME.

Adjectives

When you have finished your textbook lessons on adjectives, and
have completed your practice exercises, checking, review, and oral
or written quiz, then you are ready for your transparency activity.
Try to write the adjectives and words in italics in green.

SECRET MESSAGES

THEY LOOKED AT THE *BLOSSY* SKY.
THE GIRL HAD *GLOPPIER* HAIR THAN HER SISTER.
SHE WAS THE *BLONTIEST* LADY AT THE PARTY.

TRY ANY OF THESE *ADJECTIVES* IN PLACE OF THE
SECRET WORDS.

CLOUDY	PRETTIEST	PRETTY	BETTER
MESSY	TANGLED	PRETTIER	NICER

DO YOU GET THE MESSAGES?

CLUES TO *ADJECTIVES*:
ADJECTIVES USUALLY DESCRIBE OR TELL SOMETHING
ABOUT THE NOUN.
ADJECTIVES MAY HAVE THESE ENDINGS: *Y, ER, IEST, ED.*
ADJECTIVES CAN BE REPLACED IN A SENTENCE BY *OTHER
SIMILAR* WORDS.

By testing to see if they can substitute a known adjective like
clear, in the first sentence, and by trying out *blossy, blossier,* and
blossiest, blossy can be identified by pupils as an adjective. Avoid adjectives that could be nouns.

Adverbs

A transparency lesson on adverbs follows, but it should not be used
until your group has studied adverbs. Even individuals who have
worked ahead independently must have had some work on adverbs
before they use the Secret Messages. If you use the lesson, try to write
the adverbs and words in italics in purple.

SECRET MESSAGES

THE PEOPLE WALKED *BLAMLY.*
SHE RAN *GAMHOCKERLY* INTO THE BUILDING.

TRY ANY OF THESE *ADVERBS* IN PLACE OF THE SECRET
WORDS.

QUIETLY	HAPPILY	QUICKLY
NOISILY	NERVOUSLY	SLOWLY

DO YOU GET THE MESSAGES?

CLUES TO *ADVERBS*:
ADVERBS MAY BE *ANYWHERE* IN A SENTENCE.
ADVERBS USUALLY DESCRIBE OR TELL SOMETHING
ABOUT THE VERB.
ADVERBS MAY HAVE THIS ENDING: *LY.*
ADVERBS CAN BE REPLACED IN A SENTENCE BY OTHER
WORDS THAT ACT THE *SAME.*

Review

Your next transparency is designed to give practice in most of the
word classes covered in the preceding lessons. Since adverbs will probably not be included in the third grade work, they have been left
out of the concluding exercises. Try to color code the titles and words
in the following transparency:

HOW DO THESE NOUNS, VERBS, AND ADJECTIVES END?
WHERE DO YOU FIND THEM IN THE SENTENCES?

(orange)	(green)	(red)		(blue)
DETERMINER	ADJECTIVE	NOUN		VERB
The	pret*ty*	girl*s*		gigg*led.*
A	happ*y*	boy	was	laugh*ing.*

After you have read the titles which ask questions, reveal only the
first sentence. Discuss the answers to both questions on the first sentence before you go on to the next sentence. The pertinent endings are
italicized for you. They can be underscored on your transparency
with a special pen *after* the children discover these endings.

It will be a change of pace for everyone concerned if you have
the next transparency ready for the children to take turns filling in
on the overhead projector. Leave plenty of space in the blanks for

them to write the words. Try to write in red the nouns and the words in italics.

FILL IN THE MISSING *NOUNS.*

THE HUNGRY ————————— ATE —————————.
THE ANGRY ————————— BIT —————————.

THE YOUNG ————————————— LOOKED WELL.
THE LITTLE ———————————— CRIED HARD.

By this time, your pupils should have a very good idea of "nounness," and they should be able to work well with nouns. You have probably avoided the traditional definitions as such, but the children will arrive at a concept of *noun* through seeing and using many examples, and by studying the action and position of this word class in many sentences. Old-fashioned definitions will usually backfire; because although there is no harm in saying that nouns name things, not all words that name things are nouns. Verbs name actions and adjectives name qualities of nouns, so definitions confuse more than they clarify, if you really think them through. The important thing is that pupils learn the concept of *noun* and learn to work with nouns in noun phrases and sentences. A sample review lesson for your next transparency follows:

FILL IN THE MISSING *VERBS.*

THE BOY ——————————————— HOME.
THREE GIRLS ————————————— ROPE.
THE DOG ——————————————— HIS FOOD.
THE MAN ——————————————— A LETTER.
THEY ——————————————— THE DOOR.

In your discussion on verbs be careful to keep to the simple present tense at first. Then discuss the past tense endings. It is hard to avoid saying that the verb tells some particular thing that the subject does. Do not present this as a definition, as it will cause you trouble with words like *seem*. The main idea is to get the concept of what a verb does, and where it usually is in a sentence. To achieve this, use many examples and much practice. Children will be led to identify verbs as one of the first few words found in the predicate, and that is enough to be able to work with them.

A similar practice lesson can be presented on the overhead projector for adjectives:

FILL IN THE MISSING *ADJECTIVES*.

THE ——————— GIRL COMBED HER HAIR.
THE ——————— CAT ATE HIS BREAKFAST.
THE ——————— BOYS PLAYED BALL.

By this time you have discussed kernel sentences, and the fact that every simple sentence like this must contain either a verb or a form of the word *be*. Review the position of the abjective following a form of *be* in a kernel sentence. Remind pupils that other structures besides adjectives may also follow a form of *be*.

The following transparency lessons, called *Where Are They?* and *How Do These Nouns, Verbs, and Adjectives End?* have been used together as an effective bulletin board. This will be mentioned later, with ideas for displaying it dramatically. Keep to your color code consistently.

WHERE ARE THEY?

DETERMINER	ADJECTIVE	NOUN	VERB	NOUN
The	good	boy	ran	home.
The	hungry	cat	drank	milk.
The	curious	child	read	books.

HOW DO THESE NOUNS, VERBS, AND ADJECTIVES END?

DETERMINER	ADJECTIVE	NOUN	VERB	ADVERB
The	old	dog	walk*ed*	slowly.
The	beautiful	horse*s*	ran	well.
The	funny	clown*s*	fell	down.

As you can see, this easy repetition in a slightly different form will give the pupils a feeling of successfully accomplishing the identification of word classes. It is done quite painlessly, with gentle reminders of the clues to identification learned earlier. Let's hope that the common horror of grammar will be a thing of the past.

Be a Detective—Bulletin Board

To convert these two transparency lessons into a large, interesting bulletin board, use the following title and gimmicks. Call it *Be A Detective,* and to carry out this theme to the hilt, draw footprints, detective hats, question marks, and magnifying glasses. Color them, cut them out, and pin them in a scattered fashion near the title, and along the sides and bottom of the bulletin board. Never be prosaic, if, with a little imagination, you can make it exciting. Be sure to allow the children to do most of the work on the bulletin board. It is not suggested as a means of saving you work, although this will be delightful. The reason why pupil participation is a necessity goes back to the same need for experiences in all learning. By actively participating in the creation of the bulletin board, the pupils find it becomes part of them, so their involvement leads to learning. It should never bother you to present a slightly crooked, very finger-smudged bulletin board to your school public. If you always remember your Number One responsibility, the child, you'll take pride in this creation of his, which you've helped with. Anything too slick and perfect, done by the teacher alone, has questionable educational value. Our goal is to involve, excite, and teach children without tension, and if we never forget it, we won't worry about how our group's efforts look compared to some perfection you might see posted down the hall. We're not in the schools to impress each other, and anyone who is really experienced in evaluating teacher and pupil performance will regard highly this imperfect display.

Decoding Nonsense Sentences

Now the children are ready to go on to more difficult nonsense sentences. If you would like to have your group preview them, have these next materials as separate posters on the bulletin board for a few weeks before presenting them. Don't talk about them, but if you're asked, tell the class, "Figure them out. They're simple nonsense."

Using the signal or clue of function words to identify parts of speech, try this transparency:

THE *GROBE* WAS *BLICKING* THE *BOMTERS*.

The determiner, or function word, *the* will mark the nouns *grobe* and *bomters*. Pupils will soon learn that *was*, *were*, and *have* are clues to the verbs which follow them.

The position of words in a sentence serves as a clue. Your detectives may identify the underlined nonsense words by *where* they are:

A DIRTY *BLANTZ STILED* THE *BLOP*.
GLOOBY IS A *GLERB*.

When you finally do discuss the following nonsense sentence, read it aloud slowly, allow pupils to laugh at it, and join in too. It really does sound silly. Put as much expression into it as you can. Say *skorked* as though it was followed by an exclamation point.

WHEN THE *SLOOPY WAMTUPPER* HAD *LOOFED*
THE *STRAMBIX*,
THE *RALLOPASH SCOMED* UP HIS *FLIBBLES* AND *SKORKED*.

When the mirth subsides, get down to business. You may have a few eager beavers waving hands in the air, but you'll want everyone to understand this and discover the word classes together with you. Ignore the hands for a minute and help the people who really don't understand what the poster is getting at. Never tell them the answers. Guide your class into figuring them out by themselves, giving them clues and broad hints. Watch to see more hands going up. Mention the various clues presented earlier to help identify nouns, determiners, verbs, and adjectives in a sentence. Remind the children of position in the sentence, endings, and a word to follow; all will help. By now most of your people are ready to fully participate, so call on different pupils to analyze the nonsense sentence. Take it one part at a time. It might be easiest to locate the determiners in *When the sloopy wamtupper had loofed the strambix*. It should be simple for them to find *the* in two places. You could then ask, "Where are the nouns in this section?" The only possible difficulty could be if they think *sloopy* is a noun as well as *wamtupper* and *strambix*. This is an excellent opportunity to say that nouns in a list are separated by commas. Since two nouns would not be together otherwise, ask, "What word would be very near a noun, possibly tell something about it, and may end in *y?*" These clues should be enough to help identify *sloopy* as an adjective. The final test is to try out other known adjectives in this slot. It seems to make sense to say *the good wamtupper,* or *the small wamtupper.* It fits.

Next, read the section of the sentence again, and look for the word class which names *loofed*. If your pupils don't get it on their own, and some won't, then ask, "If the *wamtupper* had *loofed* the *strambix,* isn't it *doing* something to the *strambix?*" This should be enough. If not, point out the *ed* ending and the fact that *loofed* follows a special word *had*. The children will now be reminded that *loofed* must be a verb. Then try out a known verb like *cleaned*. It makes sense, of a sort. *The sloopy wamtupper had cleaned the stram-*

bix. This follows a natural order of words which children got accustomed to long before they came to school. Somehow, things can sound right to them when the words are in a correct order that they're used to.

Now let's go on to the rest. It can be a very relaxing kind of lesson. The lighthearted nonsense word approach tells the children that it's all right to laugh a little and enjoy this. Ask for the determiners in *the rallopash scomed up his flibbles* and *skorked*. They'll find *the* easily enough, but may need a bit of guidance to remember that *his* is a determiner. It sounds like, and is, a pronoun, and may confuse them for a minute. It's best to deal with it and clear up the confusion as soon as possible, rather than avoid this determiner. A very fine test of a determiner is to use it like this: *The what? His what? A what?* It fits in structurally with other determiners as being logically followed by a noun, so it will sound right to children. By now they'll find it easy to remember that if it tests in *The what?* or *His what?* then the *what* involved must be a noun. Once *rallopash* and *flibbles* are identified as nouns, the next step is to ask what kind of word would do something to *flibbles* and then do something else like *skorked?* If the children don't recognize *scomed* and *skorked* as verbs, patiently remind them of the clues discussed earlier. Look at the *ed* endings. A final test is to substitute known verbs in these two slots, to see how they work. The *rallopash trimmed* up his *flibbles* and *laughed*. The group will agree that this makes some kind of sense. If you like, you can change the entire sentence into English now, using known nouns, verbs, and adjectives. It's a great lesson, and may inspire you to go on with more nonsense work, which, you'll probably agree, makes much more sense than many things we do.

Another exercise could follow this. Write this nonsense paragraph on the board and have pupils *translate* it into an English story. Suggest that they circle certain nonsense nouns such as *strook,* which remain the same, to achieve continuity and meaning:

ONE DAY A *STROOK BLORBED* INTO A *BOOL*. NEAR THE TOP OF THIS *BOOL* WAS A VERY *SLATIOUS BLOBBERWORT*. AS EVERYONE KNOWS, *STROOKS GRABBLE BLOBBERWORTS*, ALTHOUGH *BLOBBERWORTS* NEVER *LOOBER STROOKS*. THIS *BLOBBERWORT* WAS *IFFY* AND RATHER *CLANFUL*. IT HAD A *RILLOUS FALE* ON ITS *RANDIX*. THE *STROOK* WAS QUITE *ANULOUS*. IT *RORKED* THE *SPOLE* OF THE *BLOBBERWORT* AND *STRILLED* IT *AMFULLY*.

COMPOSE NONSENSE RIDDLES

Writing a nonsense riddle can be a st´mulating exercise. Show the example like the following before you a k the class to compose their own.

WHAT I WOULD DO IF I HAD A *TRAMLITZ*
(PLURAL: *TRAMLITZES*)

The paragraph that follows this title describes the *tramlitz* and its function, but with enough nonsense words included so that it becomes a riddle. The class guesses what it is, using a picture of the *tramlitz* drawn on the board.

> IF I HAD A *TRAMLITZ* I WOULD BE VERY HAPPY. IT'S NOT ANYTHING LIKE HAVING A *ZOOBYFLAM*. I HAVE A *ZOOBYFLAM* THREE YEARS OLDER THAN I. WHEN WE WERE VERY LITTLE WE OFTEN *BOOLED*, BUT NOW WE GET ALONG QUITE *ZAN*. IF I HAD A *TRAMLITZ* WE COULD TAKE TURNS DOING THE *TROOLIES*, AND I COULD USE HER *ZOBES* IF WE WERE THE SAME SIZE.

In writing their own riddles, simple sketches could accompany them. They could be used as class exercises, or pupils could switch riddles with their neighbors.

Many games and exercises can be composed by teachers to fit classroom needs. Some, like *Switch*, need extensive preparation to make the word cards, but they may be used for many years. Although commercially prepared games have their advantages, in these changing times some of the best lesson materials in linguistics will come from the teachers themselves.*

CHECKLIST

Use word games such as *Switch* and *Phonic Rummy* to give practice in word families and phonics.

The test-pattern approach means testing a known word class in a slot in a sentence to see if it fits the word pattern, in order to identify similar unknown words.

Decode secret messages with your group, using nonsense words.

---

* Reprinted by permission of the National Council of Teachers of English, Rosalind Ashley, "Linguistic Games and Fun Exercises," *Elementary English*, Vol. XLIV, No. 7, November, 1967, p. 765.

Look for clues or signals in these nonsense words and their position in the sentences as a means of discovering the structure of sentences and analyzing their parts.

Play with nonsense riddles and compositions.

Vary your textbook lessons and oral language practice with transparency activities allowing pupils an opportunity to participate actively.

Make your own transparencies by preparing pencil or typed originals.

Surround your class with language posters and bulletin boards which *they* have helped to create.

Color coding your lessons is a way to dramatize and help remember differences in word classes.

Determiners *the* and *a* are clues to nouns, and always come before nouns.

Nouns may end with *s, es, s'* and *'s.*

Nouns are often used without determiners.

Verbs are in the predicate, and follow the subject in the sentence.

Verbs may have the endings *ed* and *ing.*

Verbs may follow words like *was, were, have,* or *had.*

Adjectives are usually near nouns.

Adjectives may have the endings *y, er,* and *iest.*

Nouns, determiners, verbs, adjectives, and adverbs can be replaced in a sentence by other words that act the same way.

Give review lessons, using as much variety as you can.

Avoid definitions, but let the children learn word classes through using them.

Remember the two main clues to nouns, verbs, and adjectives: *Where are they in the sentences?* and *How do they end?*

6

Resolving Common Problems in Language Usage

What does usage mean? It means the way words are *actually* used in our country, not the way some grammarian says they should be used. Increasingly, the language arts skills are being taught with the idea of language in action. The correct use of language is now our goal, and formal rules of grammar are no longer emphasized for their own sake.

In the case of a child who speaks a kind of English very different from that used in school and textbooks, we must treat him as though he needed to learn a second language, and not reject his natural way of speaking as being wrong. He may be copying the every-day speech he hears at home, and it would hurt him to think that the school and his teacher look down on it. Even if his parents speak the same kind of English that is used in educated circles, the language a child uses varies to fit the place he's in. He will copy the speech of his friends, and he will use a more informal, slang-type of English when he is with them. When he must make a choice, he will usually prefer to speak the language of his peers, so it is useless to insist on formal, standard English at all times. The best way to handle this situation is to tell him that he will need a special, more exact kind of English which follows certain rules, for school work and letters. He must be equipped to use it when he needs it, and exposure in school to his teacher's mode of speaking, and to textbooks and written practice, will usually accomplish this satisfactorily. It would be very harmful to reject his natural speech, as he would take it as a personal rejection of himself and his background. We cannot impose our cultural or class prejudices on a person from another social class or age group.

All we can do is show him that a special type of language is going to be necessary for success in all adult, business, or educational circles, and teach him how to use it. If he is able to work with it when he needs it, he will have two satisfactory languages to use, and can judge when the use of one or the other is more appropriate for his needs.

In the classroom we teach correct usage primarily by example. Our school language is standard English, and the children learn it by listening to us and copying our mode of speech. Our textbook lessons and written demonstrations use this kind of language, giving still more practice.

Aside from our constant example, we can help our pupils remember to use the formal, more correct way of speaking by reminding them in a pleasant, casual manner when they use their playground English in the classroom. The main thing is our attitude toward their other language. This might happen once in a while:

"Mrs. Ashley, I don't got a book!" the boy reported.

I smiled at him. "You don't have *what?*

"I don't *have* a book." I gave him one, as he grinned back at me.

If the purpose of language is to communicate, then this child did well. He let me know right away that he needed a book. However, the task of the teacher is to improve a pupil's spoken and written language in the classroom, so that he is able to use the standard English that educated people speak and write when he needs and wishes to do so. Since all educated people say "I don't have," then this is what is being used, and it is called correct. His "I don't got" can only be called incorrect by today's usage in schools, books, business, and government. His way of saying it may be the correct way for him on the ballfield. We can call his usage incorrect in our classroom, but it would be incorrect to ever call it wrong.

> Language changes constantly. People living in the United States in the middle of the twentieth century do not speak the English of Chaucer or of Shakespeare. They don't even speak the English of Woodrow Wilson. . . . *Silly* once meant *holy,* and the pronoun *you* could once be used with a singular verb form, as in *Was you ever in Baltimore?* Today we must say *were you.*
>
> Since language changes this much, no one can say how a word "ought" to be used. The best that anyone can do is to say how it *is* being used.
>
> . . . .
>
> Some words are used differently in different parts of the

country, but each use is respectable in its own locality. Some variations are peculiar to a trade or profession.*

Two changing usages were chosen at random for informal studies; the use of *who* or *whom*, and *can I?* or *may I?*

WHO OR WHOM?

If English followed the rules of Latin grammar we would use the form *whom* whenever the word was the object of a verb or preposition and the form *who* (or *whose*) in all other situations. But this is not the way these words are used in English.

Sentences such as *Whom are you looking for?* and *Whom do you mean?* are unnatural English and have been for at least 500 years. Eighteenth century grammarians claimed that this form ought to be the one used, but Noah Webster vigorously opposed this theory. He wrote: *"Whom did you speak to?"* was never used in speaking, as I can find, and if so, is hardly English at all.". . .

The literary tradition was with Webster and against the Latinists and this use of *whom* never became standard English. Today the form *who* is preferred when the word stands before a verb, as in *Who did you see?* The form *whom* is required when the word follows a preposition, as in *To whom did you speak?* but this is an unnatural interrogative word order. The form *whom* may be used, but is not required, when it follows the verb, as in *You saw whom?* A few people habitually observe the eighteenth century rules of grammar, but this is likely to be a disadvantage to them. To most of their countrymen, the unnatural *whom's* sound priggish or pretentious.†

So, the unnatural *whom* will probably be used less and less, except in the case of the relative pronoun. You might wish to give the following survey to your class to precede your discussion of the changing usage.

Select the one best word in the parentheses by underlining it.

1. (Who Whom) are you looking for?
2. (Whom Who) did you speak to?
3. (Whom Who) did you see?
4. To (who whom) did you speak?

When *whom* is used in sentences such as *They are workers whom we feel are underpaid*, it is really not as correct as *who*, but either form is really acceptable to most people.

---

* Bergen and Cornelia Evans, *A Dictionary of Contemporary American Usage*, (New York: Random House, 1959), pp. v. vi. vii.
† Evans, *A Dictionary of Contemporary American Usage*, p. 556.

MAY I? OR CAN I?—QUESTION IN INFORMAL SURVEY

The word *may* is used at times to express the possibility of something happening.

> *May* is also used to ask for or grant permission, as in *May I come in?* Some grammarians claim that *can* should never be used in a sentence of this kind, since *can* asks about what is physically possible and not about what is permissible. Actually, this question takes us out of the realm of language and into the intricacies of politeness.*

There is a great difference in meaning between the ability to do a thing and the permission to do it. In addition, most people make value judgments about others and place them in social and educational classes, using their speech as a criterion, so I chose the controversial usage *can I?* which is often used instead of *may I?* when asking permission, for a small, informal usage study.

QUOTATIONS OF TEN ANSWERS IN INTERVIEWS

The following answers are the results of ten interviews with my family, friends, neighbors, classmates, and a stranger working next door. This is not a random sample. A brief description of the persons interviewed and a direct quotation of each answer will be stated. The question was, "How do you feel about it when someone asks permission to do something by saying *Can I?* instead of *May I?* The two teachers interviewed were also asked what they did about this usage in their classrooms.

1. *Homemaker No. 1. High school graduate, female, married, two children.*
   "I wish the schools would teach people how to talk. My children don't talk good English. They should ask properly."

2. *Homemaker No. 2. College graduate, female, married, two children.*
   "It's important to me. I always correct my children by saying the correct word, but they don't always make the mistake. They know it, and they try to remember it to please me. I assume they're learning correct usage at school."

* Evans, *A Dictionary of Contemporary American Usage*, p. 81.

3. *Sales executive. One year of college, male, married, two children.*
"It's very important. What will people think of them if they don't know the difference?"

4. *Production manager. College graduate, male, married, three children.*
"When I hear *Can I?* that grates me! I abhor improper rhetoric!"

5. *Store owner. High school graduate, male, married, two children.*
"I'd never hire anyone who spoke like that. We like to have people who give a nice impression."

6. *Landscape gardener. Two years of high school, male, single.*
"Sure, I heard of it. I'd like to help you, lady, but I don't see why one's better than another."

7. *Teacher—fourth grade. College graduate, female, married, no children.*
"No, I don't think it matters. I've got too many more important things to spend class time on."

8. *Teacher—high school, English. College graduate, female, married, two children.*
"It doesn't matter that much. There are so many real problems to correct."

9. *College student—freshman, male, single.*
"Yes, I think you've got to teach the difference. It's important that they know it. I use *Can I?* myself in informal speech, but I know its meaning, and I don't use it in writing."

10. *High school student—junior, male, single.*
"I consider it incorrect to say *Can I* in most, if not all, circumstances. These would include formal and informal writing, and formal to semi-formal conversation. Can I leave now?"

WHAT IS BAD LANGUAGE?

Robert A. Hall Jr. said, "When purists tell us that we are using *bad* or *incorrect* or *ungrammatical* language, they are simply telling us that what we say would not be acceptable in the upper social levels." Thurston Womack's study of teachers' attitudes towards debatable items of usage shows that "in general the majority of the teachers still reject most usages that published information tends to support as acceptable." I found it interesting that of the ten people surveyed in this very small survey, only the two teachers really accepted the usage of *Can I?* and understood its implications.

This study led me to read and think more about changing usages. I've changed my teaching methods, as I realize that the pupil's peer group has chosen *Can I?* and it is socially correct for him. I continue to teach *May I?* by providing a model, and as a result the child will know the socially correct usage.

SUMMARY OF USAGE STUDY ON MAY I? OR CAN I?

Homemaker No. 1	*May I?*
Homemaker No. 2	*May I?*
Sales executive	*May I?*
Production manager	*May I?*
Store manager	*May I?*
Landscape gardener	No awareness of difference.
Teacher—fourth grade	Either *Can I?* or *May I?* is acceptable.
Teacher—high school, English	Either *Can I?* or *May I?* is acceptable.
College student	*May I?*—except in informal speech.
High school student	*May I?*—except in informal speech.

AN EXERCISE IN USAGE

Try writing some of your own materials to teach usage, so you can help pupils to learn to use standard English when it is needed.

Give examples of your own local usage in differing circumstances. Have children select the correct language, keeping these things in mind:

1. Is it correct for the place?
2. What is the purpose of the communication?
3. Who are you speaking to?
4. Do they understand you completely?

DIRECTIONS: Check the correct statements.

Oral—playground—with friends, age 10	Come on, you guys!	X

Written—classroom	The life cycle of a butter-fly begins with an egg.	X
Written—letter to a friends, age 10	This is to inform you that I will be happy to attend.	____
Written—letter to an adult	I'd like to thank you for your thoughtful gift.	X

CHECKLIST

Aim for the goal of correct use of language relative to time, place, and company, rather than memorization of rules of grammar.

Treat a child's language with respect, even if he uses a kind of English different from the standard, as it is emotionally associated with his home, parents, or peers.

Try to teach standard English as a second language needed for school, writing, and possible adult professional life, in case your pupils do not use it as their normal way of speaking.

Use standard English as an example, as this is the best way for children to learn it.

Teach changing usage by making children aware of the importance of using correct speech patterns in appropriate social and business situations.

Keep an open mind on changing usage, as these forms are perhaps only socially incorrect at this time, and in certain situations, and may be completely acceptable in the future.

7

How to Prevent Handwriting and Spelling from Blocking Expression

No, all writing is certainly not creative. But it can be, if approached as a natural way of recording one's own thoughts and speech. Writing can become forced and stilted when teachers concentrate on artificial exercises that do not relate to children's interests, or to some lesson in which the class is or was actively involved.

All thoughts and ideas are creative in one important sense. They come from us—they are ours. The fact that they may not be original has nothing to do with the natural creativity of our own feelings and impressions. This idea of originality is probably a worry to many professional writers. They tear themselves apart with the fear, "Has this been written before? Is it fresh and new?" Children have no such worries—everything is new to them. That is why all of their writing can be called creative if we allow them the freedom to experiment with words.

Look into the ways in which handwriting and spelling block children from writing things they want to write.

Stimulate your pupils' desire to create a story by using a picture grab bag. Hint at a class newspaper and let them decide that they want one. If they happen to be the rare group that doesn't want one, drop the subject. They'll probably ask for one later, as nearly everyone wants to be published, with his name in print.

In order to keep children's writing from becoming inhibited you can use your knowledge of the things they hate—and try to avoid them.

On the positive side, you may use some game-like devices to turn

95

writing into the enjoyment it should be. There are so many ways to entice children into wanting to write. You can force some words on paper, but the process and skill are what is aimed for, not the result. Since this is the case, a few short, stiff sentences scrawled to get it over with can not fulfill any educational objectives. Pupils must enjoy and take pride in their writing in order to put something into it, and to be able to get something out of it.

Everyone who writes feels at times like a woman about to deliver a child. The urgency, pain, and ecstasy mingle. Think of this feeling when you see children struggling to produce written language. Be a midwife and help them along at times. No one can take away from their joy and satisfaction in production by a *little* bit of help. Nurse them along in their labor and help to welcome their creation.

THIS IS PRIVATE

Many of the best things that children could write are never put on paper. Why? Because of embarrassment. Some pupils will delight in telling every long, intimate detail of their family's private life, from their parents' arguments to grandpa's symptoms of indigestion after meals, and more, to the point where you sincerely wish they would stop, and sometimes you're forced to cut them short. These uninhibited few will have no trouble creating written language. When you finally stop them from talking due to lack of time, or because you want to be able to face their parents at the conference table, their words will flow on paper, if you don't block them with artificial barriers. Give thought to the others—the ones who are even reluctant to tell you about their father's occupation, and are too shy to tell the group about an exciting experience they'd *love* to share. What do you do for them? Do you leave them bottled up forever? They will not improve when they reach the embarrassments of adolescence. Now is the time to uncork the bottle and let the anecdotes and stories bubble out.

There is a way. If you live up to your part of the bargain, your shy violets will bloom privately. Announce ahead of time to your group that they have a choice of how they can write their stories, articles, or poems. All they need to do is write "Private" on a story after they fold it in two, and no one else in the world will see it but you two. This means that you will have to forego sharing a funny tidbit at your coffee break or at home, no matter how cute it is. Most important of all, no other child will see it or hear of it. At conference time your only mention of it to the child's parents will be in general terms, that you have seen examples of good creative writing, or that their child has good ideas, but needs sentence work. If you can convey this idea of privacy to the inhibited majority you'll be surprised at what they can produce. There is a natural terror of being laughed at by one's peers. To have a story dissected or analyzed before the entire group can be a trauma which a child remembers each time he sits down to write. He'll say to himself. "Oh, no—they'll laugh at that. This sounds stupid. What will they think about me?" You can guess at the result—a nice safe paper with very little on it, just in case it's read aloud, or is seen by the boy in back who always teases him.

Once you've proved that you can be trusted with their *private* stories, they'll get longer and more personal. Most children crave this one-to-one opportunity to confide in just you. Since your aim is full expression and not publication, your goals will be fully reached with the private paper which confides their emotions and their stories so trustingly. Be consistent. Have your writing conferences with them in whispers, or you'll make a farce of their confidence in you. If you go all the way with them, a few may decide later that they don't mind having a story shared with the class. When they're ready, they'll tell you. Don't force it. Be sure to remind them that they can write good stories about themselves and their feelings without telling things so private that they'd embarrass their families. It's a beautiful thing to see—this gradual loosening of restraint, and willingness to become an active participant in group life. Naturally, these reluctant ones must be protected from criticism meant as teasing, or they'll retreat into their former shells.

How to Prevent Handwriting and Spelling from Blocking Expression

Use Familiar Handwriting Style

Let's pretend that you have had one or two typing lessons and someone in authority tells you to type an original story. They may give you a strict time limit, or even worse, threaten you that they're going to mark it. What is going to be on your mind as you sit down at your typewriter? The story? Not really. You're going to be worried about how you're going to type it so that it looks well. You'll be looking at the clock and fretting about how you're going to finish it in time. If you had a thread of a story in your mind before, it's unwound and blown away by now. You have other things to think about, such as, "How do you back space?" or "Where is the *w*?"

To a lesser, but similar, degree, a child who is beginning to write in cursive writing is undergoing comparable tortures when he is told to produce a written story in a limited class period. A pupil who is having difficulty with manuscript writing may suffer the same worries.

We can alleviate children's distress and help them to the freedom of expression we all wish for. Allow the first draft of any type of composition to be written in the manuscript writing that pupils feel so much at home with, if cursive writing is at all new to them. The feeling of relief they'll experience is much like the feeling you may get when you take off a pair of tight, new shoes. Your pupils will be more at ease, and they'll write better. The distracting effect of remembering their letter heights and the shape of an *f* will be gone. Even for the few who don't care what their handwriting looks like, the process of writing in cursive handwriting slows them down and limits their free flow of thought. If children are putting words on paper in a new mode of writing, they will instinctively shorten the story because they're tired of writing. This is no time for cursive writing practice, as it won't show their best efforts anyway. What do you do about the little fellow who's even struggling with manuscript writing? How do you unblock his creativity? You can reassure him about his writing by telling him this isn't being marked, and that he is not to worry about handwriting or spelling on this first copy of his story. For severe cases of blocking due to handwriting, allow the child to dictate to a tape recorder or another child and copy the story down later. If you can, be his private secretary and work with him.

Spelling Can Stop Them

To prevent blocking because of spelling, show the class how to keep going on the first draft of a story by writing the first letter and a dash for the word they can't spell; for instance, f——— for *fantastic*.* It doesn't slow them down, and the first letter helps the children to remember the word they wanted when they have time to look it up.

---

* Viola Theman, Professor of Education, Northwestern University, Evanston, Illinois.

Does this encourage sloppy spelling habits? No. On the contrary, it prevents the usual way-off guess that would be necessary when pupils don't know how to spell difficult words. Most important of all, it may keep them from changing the better word for a lesser one that they can spell. Tell the children that all you want is their ideas, and that later on you and they will work together to improve their stories. Once they know they won't be marked, they'll relax.

The other real hindrance to creativity is a time limit. It may seem easier and more efficient to collect all stories at a specified time, but if you want your pupils' best work, allow for the fact that some need more time to produce it than others. It's a good idea to collect all of the completed stories so they won't get lost, but if you keep a list with names checked off for stories handed in, you'll know who needed more time, and it's very easy to collect their stories the next morning. You can remind them that they must not have their parents' help on the stories. Make a little joke about the parents knowing how already, so they don't need more practice.

By avoiding the pressures of a new handwriting, not knowing how to spell words, possible bad marks, and time limits, you can free pupils to loosen up and write.

USE A PICTURE GRAB BAG

Picture Selection

A grab bag makes everyone think of a party. It's fun to see what you're going to get. This interesting activity for getting pupils started in story-writing needs no more than a large paper bag and about 35 pictures. It's a formidable task to find 35 good magazine pictures the night before a creative writing session, so plan ahead, and be on the lookout for stimulating color pictures. Your main goal is to find a picture that will arouse curiosity. The child should feel some sense of familiarity with the scene, or he won't understand it enough to write about it. It should not be so complete a picture that it answers all of his questions. If a child can look at a picture of a diver chasing something, his question of "What's he going after?" may trigger his imagination to provide the answer. The picture will set the scene and give him one character, and it gets him started on producing another character, human or otherwise, and some action to explain the chase. There's no limit on what he can compose, because he's free to choose any kind of adventure and a variety of endings. So, choose your pictures with care, and remember that an illustration which will inflame the imagination of one child may leave another pupil cold. The simple every-day living kind of pictures found in ads in magazines are usually too dull for most boys. Since girls like action pictures too, if you slant the subjects towards adventure and thrills, you'll cover the interests of the entire group. Collect this picture file over a period of time, and you'll gradually improve your collection as you find more stimulating pictures and discard questionable ones.

Procedure

The best procedure for this activity is to announce it a day ahead so the class can look forward to it and enjoy it even more. The first order of business is setting a few simple rules. If you don't limit the number of grab bag chances each child may have, you'll be plagued with the dilemma of a few undecided ones who never do settle down to write, but keep coming up in the hope of getting a more interesting picture. One suggestion is to allow two grab bag chances if children wish them, but they must keep the last picture even if they prefer the first one. If you have a large enough stock of pictures to give everyone two chances, then you can allow the children their choice of the two pictures, first or second.

Structure Their Stories

Tell the class that the length of the story isn't important, but that it's difficult to write an excellent story that's very short. Mention the necessary parts of a good story: a beginning to set the scene and describe the characters; a middle part with action, leading to a climax which settles any problems the characters may have; and an ending that tells what happens to them. This is impossible to do in a short paragraph. However, warn them about going on and on, making their stories so long that the endings really do not go with the beginnings. This happens because the little authors forget the beginnings that came so long before. So, a vague statement like, "Not too short, not too long—but have a beginning, middle, and an end," may be helpful.

Relate Picture to Child's Experience

Try to settle the children down at their task so that they can all concentrate. Then you'll be ready for the few who can't get started. Let's imagine the first bewildered one as he frowns at his picture. It could be a forest scene with a hunter.

"I don't know anything to write."

After studying the picture, I asked, "Does your father hunt?"

"No," he answered.

"Have you ever read about a hunter?"

"No."

We're up a blind alley. "I'll bet you've been to a zoo." I smiled with hope.

"Sure—lotsa times."

"Well, then, choose one animal you've seen, and pretend the hunter meets one. Things could happen then."

He didn't look wildly enthusiastic, but he agreed he could write about that, and the boy went to his seat and got busy.

If that hadn't helped, you still wouldn't have had to tear up his picture in frustration. You might have given up on realism, as he couldn't relate the picture to any experience, suggesting some magical happening and remembering that anything goes.

Don't Force Things

The picture is just a starting point, and if a child leaves it entirely and enjoys writing his story, who cares?

One day a child had a picture that started absolutely nothing but a pained expression on her face. We talked about the picture and nothing happened. She looked miserable. I had an inspiration.

"Could you write a story without the picture?"

"Oh, yes!" she answered.

I took the picture and said, "Fine. Good luck with it."

The pictures, of course, are just tools. If they don't help, discard them and let the children go off on their own.

OTHER STARTERS

You may want to have separate boxes for creative writing. They can contain good starting sentences, endings, or provocative titles.

For fun, one teacher hangs up two unrelated objects like gym shoes and a carrot.* Children will have to really think to compose a story about them.

A very fine black and white film called *The Hunter and the Forest* can be shown to the class. It has no words, but the action will inspire some of the best stories your pupils have ever created, as it stimulates their emotions.† Show the film, and instead of discussing it, ask the class to write about it, writing any story they wish, and expressing any feelings they might have.† † It is suitable for any age level.

The Blob

Any device which can make children wonder is good for producing a story.

One was an ink blot on a small decal, one of the many advertising promotions available, with no writing on it. With it were some large ink blots on colored signs, saying, "The blob is coming!" These signs were hung in the room weeks ahead of the blob story day. At the time planned for this creative writing activity, a small blob decal was clipped to each sheet of writing paper and passed to the children.

"What are they?" the pupils giggled.

"You'll have to guess at that," was my only answer.

When the stories were in, I noticed that there were only a few adventures written about spilled ink, but there were many mystery stories, and a few exciting horror tales.

Perhaps you can devise some ink blots of your own on a ditto-master, and have fun with the results. The experience is so open-ended that it stimulates imaginations.

A Game

A combination game and writing exercise could be started off with a few provocative sentences that the children pretend they overheard, which give the beginning of their stories. Pupils can be provided with two characters or devise their own. Any two sentences you compose can start them off well if they present some unanswered questions. For example:

---

* Peggy Pressley, Glenview, Illinois.
† Encyclopaedia Britannica, No. 878.
†† Elise Gieser, Harper School, District 39, Wilmette, Ill.

"What shall we do? They saw us with it?"
"I don't know. Call for help on your secret radio."

If you don't want to get that dramatic, try this:
"I'm going anyway, no matter what you say."
"What will you do? You have no money."

It can be fun having the different endings read aloud by those who *wish* to. It's no fun at all when anyone is embarrassed.

CHILDREN WANT TO SEE THEIR NAMES IN PRINT

Turn It Over to Them

Ask your group at a class meeting whether they *want* to have a class newspaper or magazine. This is not a thing to impose on them. If they vote to have a periodical in which to display their writing and class news, then you have a powerful motivating device to inspire the children to write their best and to write often. One way that youngsters are very much like adults is that most of them love to see their names and stories in print. If the idea of a newspaper seems like a lot of work for you, then perhaps you're too much of a perfectionist. Accept some responsibilty for checking, be willing to run off the dittoes and help in planning, and then turn the rest over to them.

If you have a class vice-president, put him in charge of selecting staff members for the paper; one supervising the creative writing handed in by anyone, two for gathering news, another for humor, one in charge of proofreading, with a few reporting on interviews.

Is It Really a Newspaper?

Go through a daily newspaper with your class. Discuss why a weather section would be inappropriate for a newspaper that does not come out each day. Talk about the length of time needed to do a good job on the paper, to compose it, gather interviews and news, rewrite it on dittomasters, run it off, and assemble it. Three weeks will be a bare minimum. Show a magazine with stories, articles, and ads. Your group will probably agree that your periodical will be as much like a magazine as it is like a newspaper. Mention the immediacy of news printed as it happens, and your time lag due to inefficient publishing procedures and equipment, plus the time needed for creative writing efforts. Plan to have at least two class periods a week for the staff to work on the newspaper, while the other pupils do creative writing for future issues. Much extra time will also be needed.

Selecting Editors

It's not the best idea for you to appoint the two most capable people in the class to be editors in charge of the newspaper, since they don't need the practice . They're good at everything anyway. It can be an exciting experience to choose two pupils who've never been chosen for anything, for obvious reasons, and let them experience the exhilaration and the joy of editorship, as well as the hours of work, writing and proofreading practice, and responsibility. They will always hold their heads up a little higher because of it. You must accept the fact that the newspaper will not be an excellent one, but the learning involved, as two editors work with their staff to gather material, stimulate contributions, write a table of contents, check articles, and finally put the paper together, can be tremendous. The ones who need to grow most will get their one chance in a lifetime. If you feel that you must have one capable child in charge, select one who needs a challenging activity, and have him work with assistant editors who need the writing and organizing experience. One highly capable, patient editor can spark a team of average learners who function as co-editors, or co-editor, with two assistant editors.

Production

There are many methods of handling the mechanics of newspaper production. The only poor ways are those where the teacher or parents do everything. Let the pupils do the entire job. Even third-graders have done it. It does not seem to work out well when one or two young pupils try to type it up in their own way, as this puts the entire load on a few. One good method was to have some of the staff check each written story, poem, or news item. The teacher then skimmed the writing for obvious errors and returned it to the newspaper staff with dittomasters.

If contributors write neatly in manuscript writing, then the staff can share the work, copying about two items on a dittomaster, checking to see if the writing is dark enough. Have a large staff and be very patient with their mistakes, which can be scraped off by you with a razor blade. Prevent their erasing or crossing out.

No matter how often you remind pupils to take out the brown protecting sheet in the dittomaster before they write, you're bound to have someone forget, so check for that before you run off the paper. Look underneath dittomasters to see that they're dark enough to be readable. This proofreading does take some of the teacher's time, but it's such an exciting project that you'd hate to be left out of it.

Your class organization should decide on a name for your publication. The vice-president can announce a contest for the best cover illustration each month, set a time limit, and collect entries. The editors and staff, plus class officers, will select the best drawing, to be reproduced on a dittomaster for the cover. With the responsibilities divided, the paper will grow quickly, and enthusiasm will be high. Help the children to write a table of contents as you finish and number the pages.

When you have run off enough individual copies for your class and one for each of the other classes in the school, then the assembling task begins. Plan ahead for it, and have the editors and staff bring permission notes allowing them to stay late one afternoon. If you borrow a few extra staplers, and allow the staff to select a few volunteers for checking page numbers, your paper will be ready for distribution.

An excellent way for pupils to express their personal opinions on all topics, and to let off some steam, is to have a Letters to the Editor page. For topics of general school interest, your editors may want to write an Editorial page. One child suggested a Problems page, where personal problems are written, so that readers could write in to offer solutions. Allow anything except articles which would hurt someone's feelings.

There may be a few children who do not wish to contribute a story or an article for the newspaper, due to shyness, or to lack of confidence in their writing ability. Since this activity is purely voluntary, accept their refusals. You can, however, try to tempt them into drawing an illustration for the cover contest, or a picture for someone's story. If that fails too, ask the editors to round up these people to help in assembling the paper, even if they aren't needed. When the paper is passed out to all of the other teachers, the principal, and is brought home to the parents, each individual should be able to share the joy of *our paper*.

Feeling the Need to Learn

Once your newspaper has been staffed, and everyone is eager to work on his assignment, you will have an excellent opportunity to teach some main points on writing news articles, even though most of the class are probably planning on creative writing contributions rather than news articles. One way to begin is to describe some recent incident that everyone remembers. Make a list on the board, showing the main things that a reporter must include in his article, and try to fill them in as a group. When you've finished, the main work of the article is completed. This will help children to get started on articles of their own.

What happened?
Who did it happen to?
Where did it happen?
What caused it?
When did it happen?
How did it happen? Give details.

If children stick to the facts in news articles and give opinions in their editorials and letters to the editors, they will learn the function of a real newspaper. Watch for exaggerations in news stories, and nip them in the bud.

An excellent help for primary teachers in planning their first newspaper is available, called *A Primary Class Newspaper, The Language Arts in Action.* *

LETTER WRITING

Letter-writing can be approached as creative writing using a certain form, or as work-type writing. Teach the form of a friendly letter, or business letter, with a transparency model. Pupils can refer to it as they write.

Explain these purposes of letter form: the salutation is a greeting which establishes contact with the person you're writing to; the address is written to make sure that you can receive an answer to your letter.

Encourage pupils to be as natural as possible by pretending that they're talking to the person to whom their letter is addressed.

* Scott, Foresman and Co., Glenview, Ill., 1965.

Pen Pals

Try planning an interchange of materials between schools in different localities or cultures. These studies need not be limited to North American communities. However, keep in mind that the economic level of the corresponding overseas school cannot be too low, or they will be unable to correspond with you. Postage on international letters is high, and the other school may not be able to send booklets or drawings to you. They wouldn't give any reasons, but you would receive no answers—a very frustrating experience.

A truly educational and satisfying way to enjoy pen pals is to select a school within visiting distance. You could pre-plan a year-long program of letters with small snapshots, visits to each school, two field trips, and close communication between two teachers and two classes. On each field trip, for maximum contact between the two groups, try regrouping the two classes before you leave for your final destination, having pen pals sit together to really get to know each other. This project could be an effective way to increase understanding between two races, or between city and country children.

In exchanging letters and materials, it is necessary that real human values, rather than superficial ones, be conveyed. Discuss the need to talk about people, friendship, hobbies, books, sports, and scouting. If your group should differ from their pen pals, this vital fact can be a tremendous opportunity to teach your pupils to value other people who may look and speak differently, and who may write in a different style. Discourage them from bragging about material possessions which another group might not possess, as the goal is to communicate and grow closer, not to impress others. Some possessions and experiences may have no meaning for children who have never heard of them. Once your pupils get to know children of another culture, they can truly appreciate them as people. One year of letters, pictures, field trips, and visits is worth a hundred lectures on democracy and brotherhood.

Other Letter-Writing Projects

In case one of your class members moves away and must attend a different school during the school year, be sure to answer any letters he may write. Don't ask him to write, as you want the child to enter his new group enthusiastically without looking back. If you, or the entire class, should receive a letter from him, try a group letter for an answer. It can be done in many ways.

One easy method is to have a friend of the ex-classmate write the first sentence and get the letter off to a friendly start. Each class member will write about one sentence after this, and everyone will sign his name at the end. Warn against silly stuff, as it could ruin the group effort. You'll probably get a bit of this anyway, so just ignore it, and send your class letter off.

If you would like to have your pupils engage in a letter-writing project causing them to receive not only answers, but brochures, booklets, and all sorts of educational reading matter, investigate the books which list free materials available upon request. The only requirements will be a letter and a stamp. You can use a transparency model to teach pupils how to write a business letter, and you'll all have the exhilaration of receiving mail at the school, which you can all share after the recipient opens it. Two warnings: try to find a current book, so the offers will still be valid, and send away early in the year, so that the answers will all come back before June.

How to Stifle Vocabulary Growth

Most children are intelligent, and all of them have a lot of common sense about how to get along in the world. School is a new environment, and in the early years these sensible children learn many tricks for happy survival.

One of these is to use their speaking vocabularies in writing only when it doesn't get them into difficulties. Any child will soon realize that a story beginning like this is going to cause him nothing but grief:

> Their was once a fandastic giant who live in a majic castle thousants of yersago.

The usual result of this literary effort is a marked paper which looks as though it has the measles. The red pencil has crossed out, corrected, and demolished his achievement, so a smart child will simplify and shorten next time. He probably took the corrections as a scolding; or worse still, he had to look up all of those words in the dictionary. His next story may start like this:

> A giant lived in a big house.

It certainly is safer. If he continues to write in this manner he gets his story back with few red marks, no scoldings, no head-shaking over his spelling, and he doesn't have to look up any words. Life is much simpler and easier this way.

How does a teacher prevent this curling up into a safe shell? It's only human nature to seek the easy, secure way. We must deal with this natural tendency by giving children a relaxed, comfortable environment in which to write. They must know that the more effort they put in, the better their achievements are appreciated. The pupil's first draft must be respected and treasured. A few words of praise, plus a suggestion or two, if needed, should be the only red marks on this first creation.

Evaluation Suggestions

When you evaluate creative writing, try to find encouraging, constructive things to say or write. For example:

The words seemed so *right* for the story.
You're able to write much longer stories now.
You told it so clearly.
It all seems so real.
This was exciting to read.

If you must say, "I like your story," or "It's very good," try to say *why*, as it will help the child know how to write another good one. It will take a little more time, but the returns will be worth it.*

Encourage pupils to use every word they know or have ever heard of, and assure them that it's all right if the spelling is incorrect at first. Explain to them that you don't expect them to know the spellings, but you'll be very proud of them if they try these new, difficult words, so they can learn them. Say that it's your job to help them with hard words if they get stuck, and that you don't mind working with them later with the dictionary, if they can't find the words on their own. You can mention that they will find it easy to look up their own words in the dictionary very soon, and that they'll find this faster than waiting their turn with you, especially if dictionaries are kept on pupils' desks.

Adding Color

Colorful writing seldom comes by itself. You can provide the stimulus by a few comparisons. The class will catch on quickly. Write

---

* Viola Theman, Professor of Education, Northwestern University, Evanston, Illinois.

some simple descriptions on the overhead projector. Then change them to sound the way a poet would describe them.

the hot sky	the blazing sky
the hot noon heat hit us	the pitiless mid-day heat struck us
the sand	the dazzling, metallic glitter of the sand

Once you inspire children to use good adjectives (and be sure that you call them by name), help them to remember the ones they know, and lead them to use new descriptive words. You can have an enlarging oral activity by starting off with a common adjective like *nice*. Write a few good substitutes under it, and then ask pupils to provide the rest. They will, and then you can feel free to add some. When the pupils start to write, they can refer to the adjectives on the board.

Teach the value of good verbs. Write this on the board or overhead projector:

He *went* down the street.

Ask the class to change the verb *went* to a more colorful word. After they've listed theirs, write these:

vanished	whirled	limped	streaked
whipped	hobbled	ripped	stamped

Try these words out in the verb slot in the sentence, and point out how much more you know about the way this man went down the street.

Write these other examples of colorful verbs which may be useful in pupils' writing:

toss	slash	shake
dodge	weave	tremble

Enjoying Poetry

When children begin to appreciate and write poetry, teachers should expose them to E. E. Cummings' "in just—," and the idea that poetry may rhyme beautifully and musically, but need *not* necessarily rhyme. If rhyme gives them pleasure, allow pupils to indulge in it, and use it to get a feeling of rhythm.

Imaginary Diaries

Fifth- and sixth-graders will enjoy creating diaries written by characters studied in social studies, basing them upon research.

CHECKLIST

Encourage children by giving them the freedom to write their own thoughts and feelings in their best vocabularies.

Prevent inhibited writing by cooperating with absolute privacy on stories, if children wish it.

Stimulate pride in workmanship by finding something worthwhile to praise in pupils' creations.

Allow the first draft of all writing to be composed in manuscript writing for third-graders, and those who need it.

Announce beforehand that individual creative writing will not be marked—that you are just looking for general effort put forth.

Emphasize that spelling and handwriting are not important in the first draft of writing.

Show spelling short-cuts for first drafts when an unknown spelling threatens to block pupils' writing.

Collect finished papers, and allow extra time when it is needed by individuals.

Generate a tension-free atmosphere for composition.

Try a picture grab bag to stimulate creative stories, with action color pictures cut from magazines.

Help pupils who cannot get started, even with a stimulus picture, to relate the picture to their real or imagined experiences.

Teach the organization of a good story—a beginning, middle, and end.

Explain the climax of a plot, and the need for characters to have problems to solve.

Don't allow any stimulating device to get in the way of a child's expression—discard it if it isn't useful.

Starting sentences, endings, titles, unrelated objects, provocative sentences, ink blots, all may trigger good stories.

Plan a class publication for its motivating value and general educational worth.

Teach good reporting and composition methods, as children see the need of these skills.

Help to proofread and run off dittoes, but expect children to actively prepare the class publication on their own, *no matter how it comes out*.

Appoint editors who need language practice and responsibility—come what may!

Involve reluctant newspaper contributors in illustrating, sorting, proofreading, and stapling.

Use transparency letter forms for teaching friendly and business letter-writing.

Engage in real letter-writing activities as a means of teaching the skill, plus learning vital social values.

Build vocabularies by encouraging and praising first draft writing attempts.

Help with spelling and dictionaries when needed.

Compare dull with colorful writing, in order to help develop the children's taste and discrimination.

Study and enjoy the many kinds of poetic expression before children attempt to create any of their own.

8

Proofreading – Ideas for Teaching Self-Criticism

If you're a conscientious teacher and have spent an evening or week-end correcting papers, you're probably familiar with the result of your efforts. The errors that you have painstakingly corrected will probably be repeated on the next paper. You also know the reason why. When these corrected papers were returned in the morning, most of the pupils stuffed them in their desks. (One has to say "stuffed," as most desks need cleaning, and the only way to put a paper in is to stuff it in.) If a few children sneaked their marked work into the wastebasket, you didn't catch them at it. Don't even try to imagine how many papers reached home safely. In this case, when you go on to your day's scheduled lessons, your previous evening's labors are being wasted, and the written lesson that the children did the day before is partially wasted, because they never found out how to improve it, or what was correct, and what was incorrect.

There are other alternatives, apart from leaving the papers un-marked. One half-measure might be to devote five to ten minutes each day, varying with the complexity of the papers being returned, for the pupils to read their papers. This works with some of the chil-dren, but most of them seem more interested in the new work planned for the day than in reading an old paper from yesterday. The other choice available to the teacher is to spend whatever time is necessary to read the marked papers, discuss the corrections, and answer ques-tions. The children don't seem to care about these papers any more. They don't want to rehash old stuff. They, and the teacher, tend to rush through it as something to get over with. Going over the teacher's marking the next day doesn't seem to be the answer. What is?

The corrections that mean the most to children are those made by the pupils themselves, immediately after completing and checking the work. At that time they *care* how they did on the lesson, and they're curious to know the correct answers. The children clap over correct ones, and sigh and moan over mistakes. The entire atmosphere is different. Since the original reason why we chose to mark pupils' work at home rather than do it in class was to save on teaching time, we've gained nothing if we devote the same time to discussing the teacher's marking, a day too late. It seems obvious that the best educational returns will come from the immediate reinforcement, positive or negative, of marking following the lesson, with the corrections made by the children themselves. Teachers will find that they have more free time at home for lesson planning, and will be more refreshed and creative the next day. The pupils will know the results of their efforts on the same day, and they can learn the corrections immediately. Now it doesn't really matter where they stuff their papers. The educational job of the marking is done. The only value the marked papers have now is to keep the pupils' parents informed of their child's progress.

Weren't We Talking About Proofreading?

What does paper marking have to do with proofreading? Everything. We have to teach children how to mark, just as we must teach them to accomplish other important school tasks. Let's name some of the elements involved in successful marking. The main thing a child must learn is how to find mistakes. This might seem too obvious to mention, but visual scrutiny is an activity that requires skill and practice. It is a major cause of reading errors in reading achievement tests. To mark well, a pupil must look at every letter in a word, as well as its general pattern. Good marking can be learned by most children, but it takes time and practice. Aside from looking at a word, the child must take the time to compare it with the correct answer provided on the chalkboard, the overhead projector, or answer book. As you know, nearly all of your pupils are in a great hurry. They have nowhere to go until three o'clock, but they're in a frantic rush anyway. They don't have time to compare carefully. This last element is the most difficult to accomplish in marking. You'll find that devoting enough time to the job is the part of proofreading or marking that children will resist to the last. Checking of work and marking are nearly alike.

Since proofreading and marking are so closely related, we should analyze how they are alike and how they differ. They're identical except for one very important factor—the answers. In proofreading, a pupil checks for mistakes in order to correct them, but he doesn't always know a mistake when he sees one. When he marks he does nearly the same thing. He checks for mistakes in order to make corrections and learn what he didn't know before, only now he has the answers in front of him.

A Proofreading Conference

We can save our pupils a great deal of work, and enable them to feel the satisfaction of achieving success in their lessons, by helping them to find these same mistakes *before* they mark, rather than during the marking. Naturally, in many cases they don't know the answer, so they can look right at an incorrect response and not recognize it as such. Many, many times this is not the case, and if pupils take the time to really look at what they've written they'll see that it isn't what they meant to write at all. You've probably had this happen often at your desk. A child has a story or a letter and you want to help him find his own mistakes.

You point to the first line.

"Let's read it together. How is it?"

He reads it silently and giggles. "I forgot a word."

"Fix it," you reply.

You lend him a pencil and he writes in a word. You read the next sentence together. "That's all right," he says.

"How about the next one?"

He reads on and grabs the pencil to put a period at the end of the sentence.

You smile at him and say, "That's much better. Here's a new word for your spelling list." You write it correctly for him and he sits down with a corrected story. He did it himself, didn't he? The only thing he didn't spot was an incorrect use of the word *there*, instead of *their*, which he really didn't know yet.

Our goal must be to help our children to grow enough so that they can do this proofreading on their own, without standing at our desk. We want them to find most of their errors, but we don't expect perfection. It's not as easy as it sounds, but we must try.

This chapter tells how one group keeps alert by watching for their *teacher's* mistakes each day—and how she keeps making them! A proofreading check-off list called a *Mistake Hunt* is reproduced for you to use, as well as ideas on specific proofreading lessons which also teach concepts from other curriculum areas. There is nothing more frustrating than to hear that you haven't written a complete sentence when you don't know what a sentence really is. Ways to show pupils what a sentence is are shown. Get your pupils accustumed to looKing four mis-steaks. It Kan be very amusing,

BRIGHTEN THE DAY BY CATCHING TEACHER'S MISTAKES

It was a balmy spring afternoon. The children were dreaming of recess. I was explaining accented syllables. Perhaps I was dreaming of recess, too.

Suddenly, the children's faces were alert and smiling. At least fifteen hands were waving. What wonderful thing had awakened them?

"Mrs. Ashley, you made a mistake! You forgot to cross your *t*," someone said. I crossed it immediately and went on with the lesson. The children were intently watching now, but not, I feared, for accented syllables. Later, I thought it might be fun to see if they were still paying such close attention, so I intentionally misspelled a word. Immediately, hands went up.

This gave me something to think about. I had been disturbed because my third-graders seemed unable to discover their own mistakes. Yet, how quickly they had pounced on mine! I decided to attempt a systematic training program in proofreading by giving them practice in catching me in mistakes.

The next morning when I wrote the daily schedule on the chalkboard, I deliberately misspelled words, made incomplete letters, and omitted capitals.

By the time my pupils discovered the third mistake, they had caught on to the game, but this awareness didn't spoil their fun. They were still excited and interested. When all mistakes were corrected on the board, we began our regular lessons. The children were smiling and eager. The day had begun well.

We have been doing this every morning. The mistakes change all the time, but the game remains the same. The children often whisper ideas of new mistakes to me. I have substituted *m* for *n* so often that the tendency to mix up the two has almost disappeared from their work.

A Mistake That Backfires

I realize that it is not good for children to look at errors on the board. For this reason, I pull a map down to cover the board until we are ready to correct the daily schedule. The only mishap occurred one morning when the children were to be tested by a testing service, and I forgot to pull the map down over the board. The woman who was administering the test kept looking at the chalkboard. I knew what she was thinking, but I didn't want to interrupt. After she left, the incident became a private joke which my class shared with me.

As a follow-up to the board practice, I provide pupils with ditto sheets filled with errors, so they can gain intensive proofreading practice on their own. I believe that the children are now able to look more critically at their own written work. I have found corrected errors in their papers. The *mistake* game provides a delightful way to start the day.*

THE MISTAKE HUNT—LET THEM DO THE WORK

There has been so much emphasis put upon a free, relatively uncriticized first draft of writing, that you may be wondering when the equally important proofreading and self-criticism is taught. The first draft has been read by the teacher and an encouraging phrase or two has been written in the corner. The child receives this a day later, and has class time to read the comments and think about them. Now we may pass out a dittoed copy of a Mistake Hunt, which is a check-off list for self-improvement of written material. It is suitable as it is, once adjectives have been taught. Before that, item No. 2 must be explained fully.

---

* Reprinted by permission from *Grade Teacher* magazine. Copyright 1966 by Teachers Publishing Corporation. Rosalind Ashley. "Spotting Teacher's Mistakes Keeps Pupils on Their Toes," Vol. 84, No. 1, Sept., 1966, p. 24.

NAME_____

MISTAKE HUNT

You are going to look for *your* mistakes today. Read each thing on this list. Put a check mark on the line following each item after you have done it.

1. Read your paper to see if it makes sense. If not, add words or change it so that it says what you *want* it to say. Use this mark for adding something. ($\wedge$)   ____

2. Read through your work to see if you repeated words. Try to think of better or different ones if you can. Adjectives, which describe things, make your story more interesting.   ____

3. Did you skip a line after your title? If not, put an (X) under it to remind you.   ____

4. Read through each sentence carefully. It should have a subject and predicate. Write the correct mark at the end of it. If it, *tells* something, write a period. If it *asks* a question, write a question mark at the end. If you stop for a rest in the middle, or list things, use commas.   ____

5. Use a capital letter at the start of every sentence, on every proper name, and on all the main words of your title.   ____

6. Circle all of the words that you think have spelling mistakes. Look them up in the dictionary to find the correct spelling. Try to do it by yourself, but ask for help if you cannot do it.   ____

7. Did you indent (go in) on the first line of every paragraph? If not, put this mark to remind you. (¶) Change paragraphs with a new subject, and when someone new speaks.   ____

8. If you tell what people say, write quotation marks around what they say. These marks look like this: ("Hello.")   ____

Give the class time to read this sheet and ask questions about it. Practice using the Mistake Hunt on a sample story. Then make sure that your pupils understand their responsibility in putting a check mark after each item has been accomplished. In the case of Number

Eight on the Mistake Hunt, if theirs is expository writing, or a story with no conversation, children may check it off as read and not needed. Teach straight margins some other time, and concentrate on the main things now.

THEY HAVE EYES, BUT CANNOT SEE

Number Six may be checked off as done, and you will probably find many spelling errors in the work. Your pupils may *think* the words are correct.

This leads us to our next task, which is to check our pupils' checking. Individual conferences as they finish are the best way. If you find incorrectly spelled words, circle them. Many errors and omissions will be discovered as you quietly point to them. It's better to allow neat corrections rather than to insist on recopying without a specific purpose, when this is possible. If a child seems unaware of the meaning of paragraphing, write the mark (¶) before the place which should have been indented. A few more paragraphing lessons may be needed for a small group, or just for this individual. It is useless to make an issue at this time of a sentence fragment which is not a sentence. If the child reads it carefully and finds it satisfactory, scolding him is not the answer. An analysis or review of subjects and predicates is due.

What Is a Sentence?

The old definition of a sentence being *a complete thought* will not hold up. Linguists will joyfully point out that many phrases can be found which express a complete thought. They say something about something. A complete sentence contains a subject and a predicate. Teach each separately as one of the two parts of a kernel sentence. To be a complete sentence it cannot just *name* something or describe it. Explain to the children that this would be a subject by itself. You must *say* something about the subject—give it a predicate. A good sentence needs a specific verb which is limited with reference to person, number, and tense. The sentence must sound finished, and it will when a special verb tells something about the noun phrase, or subject. Practice in contrasting sentences with sentence fragments will be useful at this point.

Another very important clue to a sentence is the dropping of the voice to signify an ending when it's read aloud.

English Word Order

Try to give children an awareness of the fixed word order of the normal English sentence. They have been using this order since childhood. It doesn't have to be taught, as any ordering of words which changes or violates this sounds incorrect to them. English has this special pattern, as discussed in Chapter Five, under Test-Pattern Method.

<blockquote>
Correct word order: The big brown dog went into his large, freshly painted red' doghouse.
Incorrect word order: The brown big dog . . .
The dog big brown . . .
</blockquote>

We regularly change the normal sentence order of English to produce a question:

You are fine. How *are you?*

Stick to normal word order in teaching the lower grades, unless you have a special reason such as emphasis, or a poetic quotation.

Indent!

Paragraphing is difficult for everyone, not just children. Teach that a paragraph usually gives a main point or conclusion, and then elaborates on it, with examples. To help the pupils understand paragraphing, tell them what it really is. It's a convention for the convenience of the reader. It marks the divisions of our thoughts where we discuss one subject or one part of it, and it points out the organization of our story or article. No one can tell you in advance how long your paragraphs should be. Children must use common sense in not making them too short or too long.

To teach composition at all you should emphasize the importance of the topic sentence. It forms the basis for your paragraph. This topic sentence usually begins the paragraph, which is built around it, but many fine authors sometimes place it elsewhere in the paragraph. To give children a good, simple start, have them begin a paragraph with a topic sentence.

A very important use for the paragraph is to indicate dialogue. This, also, is a convention. Teach your pupils to change paragraphs with each new speaker, as indicated in Number Seven of the Mistake

Hunt, but if a speech by one speaker is very long, tell them that they may use more than one paragraph for the same speech, repeating the quotation marks each time they indent for a paragraph. Paragraphing is a very useful convention for the reader. It makes it easier for him to know who is speaking in dialogue.

Use Comics to Teach Quotation Marks

One of the more difficult concepts for young children to learn is that of dialogue being different from descriptive writing. Teachers must help them learn the difference. Pupils have seen quotation marks enclosing dialogue in books, but have taken them for granted. A more familiar enclosure for dialogue is the comic strip balloon holding the character's words. An interest-provoking lesson on quotation marks and dialogue can be easily produced from your favorite comic strip any day. The children will be delighted and you'll get a lift from doing something different. Select a familiar comic strip in which the balloons enclose complete sentences. It's best if two people are speaking to each other. Scotch tape the cut-out comic to a piece of lined paper, and write your simple directions beneath it. Run this through your office copying machine on a No. 127 transparency, and your lesson will be ready for the overhead projector. Sample directions are written below. You can fill in the names of your cartoon characters and the number of paragraphs needed:

> Read the cartoon.
> Write _____ paragraphs telling the exact words that _____ and _____ say. Place quotation marks around the words each character uses.
> Why do we need _____ paragraphs?

Before the children begin their individual work, make an oral comparison for them between the enclosing balloons and the quotation marks which do the same thing. Remind pupils that the only difference between the two is that when one character continues speaking in two comic strip frames, the quotation marks need not be repeated until he stops talking.

Allow a class period for the written work, and then check it together. Prepare another transparency, transposing your cartoon into a short story with quotation marks in the correct places. As you check together use the revelation method, uncovering one part at a time for maximum effectiveness.

Using various lessons we can teach children to proofread their own work for good sentences, paragraphs, and quotation marks. To be able to see errors in these they must have enough background information and experience to discern the correct from the incorrect.

Training for Proofreading Skill While Reviewing Science Concepts

Any science material lends itself to an exercise similar to the following. You can pinpoint errors that your individual group frequently makes.

PROOFREADING

each bee hive has its police bees, who guard against stranje bees and Keep each bee in place within the hive, Onli the wurker beez sting people. They dy after stinging/ Queen bees stay in the hive. They can sting other queens.

Certain bees air-condition the hive by fanning there wings. They stand nere the entrance And fan fresh are into the hive in summer. They warm the hive in kiold weather by buzing their wings,

One male mates with the queen. When A yung queen is developed, the old queen swarms with a group uv workers and starts a nu hive/?

Bees can be harmful becauz they sting peopl and aminals.

Bees can be helpful. Honeybees mak honey They are necessari to the pollination of many plants, including fruit treez. Only bummblebees can pollinate red clover. The pollen is necessary to these plants so new plants kan gro.

Never hesitate to point out an error during checking time if the class misses it completely. The group objective is a corrected paper. This type of lesson is best done with individual ditto sheets for each child to correct with pencil on his own. You can prepare one master pencil copy, and get a transparency and a dittomaster from it. Checking can be done together after the pupils have corrected the papers as well as they're able to.

Present a science proofreading lesson after the class has studied most of the science unit. In this way pupils will be familiar with the vocabulary and able to keep their main attention on the proofreading, rather than on the content.

Proofreading Practice

Use interesting, informative material related to science or other units for proofreading practice. However, once in a while it's amusing to work together orally on a "Horrible Example" paper which will give everyone a good laugh at its obvious errors. The end of the year might be the best time for this if you have third-graders. Make a transparency similar to or using the following lesson. Allow plenty of space between lines for written corrections. You will need to use two pages of transparencies for a lesson of this length.

Find the mistakes. Fix them.

HORRIBLE EXAMPLES

John and I were play. Me and him aint got nothing to do, so we was watchin television. just then the fire sirens blown. We knowed that we shouldnt go out and get in thu way We don't never disobey important instructions, so we watched frum the window,

Ther was an fire across The street. Kenny was tooken too the hospital in a ambulance. His mother come with him.

We brung our paper and crayons near the window. john teared a page out of a coloring book and brung it to. I done that last tine so I just drawd on paper

Reveal one section at a time, and correct it with a special pen that has brightly colored ink. Everyone will thoroughly enjoy it. Write in your own group's favorite incorrect expressions. Children who were saying the same phrases only weeks ago will howl with glee and superiority as they correct the written mistakes. This is also suitable for a written lesson with group corrections at the end.

Proofreading Used for Diagnosis

If you think about it, proofreading is much more than just checking work before it's handed in, important though that may be. Once you teach your pupils the skill of proofreading, you can use it as a diagnostic device. Children who know how to check, but do not do it, can be screened for learning disabilities. A perceptive teacher will know what language skills to reteach small groups by carefully watching her class proofreading their work from day to day.

You can personalize your instruction by groups, concentrating on specific needs as shown in pupils' writing. Separate those who need work using periods and capitals, or just address your remarks to them, letting the others listen in as review. This is best done by putting a transparency on the overhead projector, showing the type of error or omission. Allow the children to tell *you* how to correct it.

Personal Checklists

Individualize proofreading by making up a notebook page containing a checklist with personal reminders written for each child. He can refer to the list after a piece of writing, keeping his special needs in mind.

After regular proofreading lessons visual scrutiny will improve, careless habits will diminish, and children will take more pride in their written work.

CHECKLIST

Utilize the children's enjoyment in catching your mistakes to provide proofreading practice, in the hope of some transfer to their own work.

Supply a proofreading checklist to help your pupils as they proofread their written work, practicing with it together before pupils use it on their own.

Have your first checklist item be a check to see if the story makes sense, and if pupils have a group of statements which say what they meant them to say.

Remind pupils to avoid repetition by using their best *speaking* vocabularies, and learning how to spell the words later.

List reminders on punctuation, good sentences, and paragraphs.

Circling by pupils and teacher of words needing spelling correction will lead to awareness of differences in appearance between correct and incorrect words.

Expect each item on the checklist to be checked as either completed or not needed.

Proofreading skill with sentences, capitals, and periods cannot be expected until pupils really understand the difference between a complete sentence and a sentence fragment.

Teach and practice using the unique word order of an English sentence.

Give lessons and review on topic sentences and paragraphing before you expect a child to know where to indent.

Teach your pupils how to paragraph dialogue, indenting with each new speaker, or oftener if one speech is long.

Use comic strips in preparing your own transparency lessons to teach the correct method of placing quotation marks for dialogue.

Train for proofreading skill with dittoed sheets, while reviewing science concepts.

Have fun with a "Horrible Example" oral proofreading lesson, after your pupils have had many oral proofreading experiences.

Plan individual conferences to check on pupils' proofreading skills.

Diagnose for reteaching by what has not been corrected during proofreading, watching for perceptual handicaps.

Personal needs listed on an individual checklist serve as reminders for each child.

9

The Magic of Words – Suggestions for Creative Expression Using Games and Sketches

Words are so much more than the building blocks of language. They're the alchemist's tools, the mystical ingredients in a magical brew which can intoxicate, hypnotize, incite, inflame, amuse, influence, and carry away our fellow human beings. No Merlin or Houdini could have created magic more potent than that which is mass-produced by the advertising and propaganda agencies of today. It's no coincidence that a fascinating orator can be called a "spellbinder." Words, used in certain ways, can create seemingly mysterious effects.

Remember the charm of the beauty of words. Lovers have used poetry for wooing for centuries, and will continue to do so. Poetry is taught in elementary schools, not only for literary appreciation, but to give a pupil a sense of the magnificence and imagery of language well used. Alliteration and rhythm may be unknown quantities to your children, although they've probably been enjoying rhyme for years. Show them, and let them feel, the beauty of rhythmic language. Onomatopoeia (the word no one can spell), is something that should be taught to illustrate the power of words. Give the examples of *tinkle and buzz,* and then let them tell you some words that imitate the natural sound associated with the object or action.

If you've ever read the Sherlock Holmes story, "The Mystery of the Speckled Band," written by Sir Arthur Conan Doyle, then you're quite aware of the power of words to evoke fascination, horror, and fear. This is another vital aspect of language which must be taught to children, not only for their use in creative writing, but in order for them to be able to protect themselves from being influenced too much

126

by propaganda. Everyone succumbs to it in some degree, but teaching the awareness that this device can be used for more odious reasons than selling toothpaste is a necessary educational task.

Words Can Be Funny

Try to amuse your pupils with words. The pun may be lowly in other places, but in a classroom its effect can be too strong to be anything less than magic. When you use language only to spread and receive information, you're missing its many other powers to work for you. Create an atmosphere of excitement and energy in your class by using words for the unexpected fun they can create. Never be embarrassed to try a little joke or play on words. The first rule of keeping an audience is to entertain them. You teach them things as you go along, but use the good speaker's, or toastmaster's, magic formula. Amuse them first, to get their attention for what you want to do later. This does not mean that you need to start each day with, "A funny thing happened to me on my way to the auditorium. . . ." That could become trite very soon. You can exploit the *natural* humor in daily situations. Life and people can be very funny. Be ready, and help your pupils to enjoy humor. There's nothing wrong with jokes used effectively. Your group may enjoy having a joke, riddle, and cartoon file, which all of you help to maintain. A class helper can post a new joke or cartoon each day. The best humor of all is something you might just happen to say. Stop to laugh at it. A word of caution: never make fun of an individual; that causes hurt feelings.

Words of Praise

Examine the witchery of praise. Writing six little words on a child's poor, but well-erased paper, "I can see that you tried," can create a feeling of hope, rather than the negative one of "What's the use?" That's magic, isn't it? Words, to retain their potency, must be sincere. They lose their charm when it's obvious that they're not meant.

Where Do the Words Come From?

Investigate the origin of words with your pupils. Many a good teacher has happily gotten off the lesson subject to explore where a familiar word came from.

For instance, the English language borrows words from many other languages. We use the word, the spelling, and the meaning from another tongue. The French word *rendezvous* is a borrowed one. You can delight your pupils with a discussion on words which have been derived from other languages. Write the following list on the board, or on a transparency for the overhead projector. It will stimulate the pupils to contribute a few words of their own:

Word	*Language*
kindergarten	German
camel	Hebrew
rodeo	Spanish
canyon	Spanish
sugar	Persian
balcony	Italian
robot	Czechoslovakia
acrobat	Greek

Wherever possible, relate these words to others which show their meaning. The fascination increases when you mention the Acropolis in Greece and write its name for them to see. Tell pupils that the beginning of the word means *height* in Greek. The acrobat works at great heights, the Acropolis is a high hill, and the city of Akron, Ohio bears the Greek word for heights.

Let's compare English and Spanish as a means of fascinating children with language. Pupils' first impression will be how much alike they are. With the following similar words (known as cognates), you can demonstrate how English and Spanish originated in Latin. The pairs have enough similarity *and difference* to cause children to think:

English	*Spanish*
rich	rico
fresh	fresco
gun	pistola
one	uno
river	rio

You will enjoy analyzing a Spanish word like "primaverra" to show its meaning and relationship to English.

English	*Spanish*
first	prima
green	verra

Since "primaverra" is the Spanish word for "spring," the English meaning of "first green" will appeal to pupils.

The geographical names for cities, rivers, and regions are closely allied with their history, economics, and topography. The name Silver City, Arizona, tells a story. Palm Springs, California; Midland, Texas; and Big Lake, Texas all have descriptive names. The name Pacific means "peaceful." Your pupils might enjoy a map exercise of looking for interesting names which describe the place, tell how the people earn their living, or tell of its past. A city in Mexico has the interesting name of Aguascalientes. Point out that *agua* means "water" in Spanish, and *caliente* means "hot," so this place must be similar to our Hot Springs, Arkansas. Whenever you mention a place name, write it so pupils can see the spelling and make mental connections with other words. This may even inspire children to learn Spanish or some other language. Detroit, Michigan signifies strait, or narrow place, in French. Many places are named for individuals, but it is interesting to learn that the Lincoln counties in Georgia, Kentucky, Missouri, North Carolina, and Tennessee are named for General Benjamin Lincoln, an officer of the Revolution, and not for Abraham Lincoln.* It's quite logical, if you think about it.

Any good Spanish language manual can help you develop a wonderful lesson on place names which will teach a lot of geography as well as language, and you don't have to know a word of Spanish.

Buenos Aires	good air
Costa Rica	rich coast
Los Angeles	the angels
Rio Grande	big river
Puerto Rico	rich port
Ecuador	equator
Las Vegas	the meadows

There are many more, and your pupils will want to watch for them in books, as well as maps, and share them with the class. It might be good to point out that in the case of Las Vegas there are certainly no meadows there now, although the area is flat. This is a good chance to bring in the climate and rainfall problems of this area, and the ever-changing land forms through long periods of time.

Weave social studies and language lessons together by investigating the different meanings that words may have in various cultures.

---

* Lewis H. Chrisman, "Teaching Values in the Study of Place Names," *The Journal of Geography*, Feb., 1934, pp. 61-6.

The ancient Egyptians used *pyramids* as burial tombs for royalty. The pyramids came to a point, and formed the concept we have of the meaning of the word. However, in Middle America, of the many *pyramids* to be found left from antiquity, only one is known to have been used as a tomb. The other structures were built in honor of their many gods. Another interesting sidelight on this word is that the shape of the Middle American pyramids found in present-day Mexico is quite different from those in Egypt. The latter taper up to the top, but the Mexican pyramids have flat tops, and do not come to points. They also have stairs cut into their sides. So, one word can mean two similar but different structures.

The enjoyment of language is not limited to the language arts, as you can see. It spreads to every other part of the curriculum to enrich and enliven it.

The Spell of Stories

Words, properly used, can draw a picture and take your children to any place you care to bring them. If your spell is slightly weak, they may not really arrive there in their imagination, but they'll be able to shut their eyes and picture the place. For example, when you want to bring your class to the country of Iraq, use every magic carpet at your disposal. Play the recording *Scheherazade** softly in the background. Tell them about the sultan's bride in the *Arabian Nights* who saved her life by telling wondrous stories. Read the story of "Sinbad, the Sailor" aloud. Describe the bazaars, and the farms near the rivers. Show or draw a picture of a minaret; pretend to listen to the gossip of the men in the coffee houses by helping a few boys dramatize a scene, with the men going to the coffee houses after dinner. Then bring the children to the desert with you by giving each one a date to taste. Let them feel the dry heat in their minds, endure the thirst mentally, smell the camels in their imagination, and actually feel the gritty sand between their teeth. If you're lucky enough to achieve this, please allow them time for drinks after this lesson.

Words with Props

Show pupils what the printed language looks like if you're studying Greece to help them realize the meaning of the expression, "It's

---

* Rimsky-Korsakoff, Vienna Tonkuenstler Symphony Orchestra, 33⅓ R.P.M., Plymouth, P12-15.

Greek to me." The Greek alphabet is so different from ours that it will fascinate your group to see the Greek written language. Use a pocket travel book to try out a few phrases. They're written out phonetically for you, so you can say them. Try to find a Greek person to speak to your group about his homeland. You might even be fortunate enough to obtain someone who can show you slides of Greece as he talks, as many travelers make slides and love to show them. Find out whether your school has a Community Talent Pool, with volunteers willing to get demonstrations, lessons, and talks for the children. Don't fail to borrow a recording of Greek dances, and get someone to show you one simple step. The last 15 minutes of an afternoon would be ideal for this. Once your group has danced to the thrilling Greek music they'll have a new feeling for the country. (They'll also be so excited that they'll be unable to do anything else.) Tell the children about the sweet honey desserts that the Greek people love. Perhaps they could ask their parents to get some for them to taste. Show pictures of the classic Greek architecture, relating it to the many famous public buildings in our country which are patterned after the Greek styles. Display objects such as dolls dressed in Greek costumes. Many parents travel and bring these back as souvenirs. Let a committee prepare a bulletin board on Greece, using postcards, pictures, reports, and Greek newspapers. A sound film will add to the experience too. Read the exciting Greek myth about Apollo and his son, Aesculapius—they'll thrill to the adventure of his hot, wild ride across the sky.

As you can see, along with the sorcery of words, you may use a few props. Music, drawings, costumes, dolls, food, slides, and films can increase the spell of your words.

So, as chief magician in charge of education, use every magic word you can in your potion for learning and stimulation. The best spice of all to give your words feeling and zest may be nothing more at times than a smile. Words can't be dull—only the way people use them may be. Words can create magic, and so can you.

You'll enjoy learning a creative word game which can be extended into an all-school activity if you wish. A vocabulary game is an exciting and practical way to introduce any unit, and it's especially helpful before a science unit. Many word games have double values as vocabulary builders and spelling practice, so don't begrudge time spent on them once in a while. Some old and new favorites are reviewed here with their simple rules. Use root words as the basis for many activities, especially in understanding new, difficult words. To help children really understand root words, use an audiovisual lesson with a simple drawing.

How to Develop Word Power in a Lively Bulletin Board Game

"In this game we write a word to look like its meaning." To illustrate, I wrote *small* so tiny that it couldn't be read on the chalkboard. Then, with colored chalk, I wrote *colorful* with each letter a different color. The word *slant* was written to look like this:

SLANT

Their hands were up by then. One frantic waver contributed "shaky." He ran up to write it.

SHAKY

The fun continued, as one of my slowest third-graders delighted us with:

DRUNK

I showed them a few more, but they weren't needed:

CORNER LOOK off Kick

Let the Whole School
Participate

As the inspiration increased rather than diminished, I decided to use this game as a hall bulletin board, so that other classes could participate.

We had a bulletin board committee for each month. I wrote the poster explaining the game, and they did all the rest. This committee cut 2" x 6" tagboard cards and wrote some of the best words from our class game on them. They stapled these up on the hall bulletin board with the poster and a small card saying *A Game*. A hosiery box was stapled up with two yarn supporters tied to holes in the box. Blank cards were placed in the box. Another poster invited the rest of the school to play by writing their ideas on the cards, giving their names. We waited for contributions.

Instead of contributions we had crowds. Each time our class passed the bulletin board during the school day there were at least two or three children there, reading the cards. Before and after classes it was mobbed. Then the blank cards were gone. By the next day we were swamped with word cards and little scraps of paper, because the tagboard cards had been used up.

The bulletin board committee worked like beavers all month trying to keep the box filled with blank cards, as we didn't want to post scraps of paper.

Before class every day my pupils had the fun of examining the entries. There were so many that I chose only the best to show them, or our day would have been devoted to just this. They helped to choose the winners from the cards I shared with them, and the committee pinned them up in their spare time.

As expected, by the end of the first week the bulletin board was full, and we received permission to put some word cards up on the wall near it. We rejected repeats and many good cards in the interest of space. In our room we had a large box of unused entries. Obviously, some enthusiasts were devoting much energy to writing word cards.

By this time the other teachers on our floor were jokingly complaining of the time taken in their rooms while their pupils wrote word card entries. One teacher solved this by giving them five minutes every morning and afternoon to do this.

The children in my room took a personal satisfaction in the popularity of *their* game. Everyone involved had a great deal of fun with it. I'm sure their vocabularies were enriched. I can never know how their creativity was affected, but I can hope.*

OTHER WORD GAMES

Even the best of teachers have a few clock-watchers in a room. The danger signal, however, is when *you* too begin to watch the clock, hoping that dismissal time comes soon.

Be flexible enough to change the pace immediately. Don't let your lesson plan book rule you. After all, you wrote it. Scrap the elaborate lesson you've planned and have it tomorrow. There are diminishing returns as the afternoon progresses. If you're getting bored, just imagine how your class feels. This same activity postponed until the next day will have more zest and attention when the mood is right, so don't waste it on an unreceptive group.

This is the time for a word game. Here are a few.

Catalogs

A word game called *Catalogs* is an exercise in quick thinking and vocabulary practice. Choose one child to be leader. He will announce a letter of the alphabet; for example, *d*. In a given amount of time, such as two minutes, the other players must make a list of all of the objects in the room that have names beginning with the letter *d*. The first one that would come to mind would be *desk,* followed by *door*. This could be a lot of fun. Then the one who had the longest list would become the leader and choose a new letter for the group to work with.

Funny Rhymes

You can play with rhymes that remind children of common things. Try combining two rhyming words to see if you can think of something. The object of this game is humor and vocabulary enrichment. It will take some time, and if the children can't think of anything, just smile and say, "Forget about it." They won't, and the next day you'll probably get a few good ones that they've figured out. Some examples follow:

---

* Reprinted by permission of *The Instructor*. Rosalind Ashley, "Fun With Words," Vol. LXXVII, No. 8, April, 1968, p. 120.

television	free see
refrigerator	hold cold
umpire	call ball
cooking	hot pot
telephone	hire wire
wig	spare hair
brat	wild child
landscape	green scene
toll road	pay way
comedy	gay play

Homonym Contest

Homonyms are excellent materials for games. You might want to have a contest to see which pupil can think of the most pairs of homonyms.* (One child contributed 176 pairs.) Get them started with a few.

| pair | pear |
| to | two |

INTRODUCE A SCIENCE UNIT WITH A VOCABULARY GAME

There are many activities and games that you can create to fit a specific science unit. Since your goal is to get the pupils acquainted with a new, special vocabulary in an interesting manner, you will assume that they do not know what any of the words mean, except for a few familiar easy ones which you include deliberately. You want to tell your pupils the new meanings in a way that they will remember, so provide an activity in which they try to match words with simple definitions by guessing. This will require a relaxed, informal attitude, so that children learn from the words they don't know, rather than get upset by them.

Since nearly everyone is guessing, it's more like winning a game than like doing well on a quiz, and the losers aren't going to really care too much. Insure this by announcing that you couldn't possibly expect children to know these new words before you teach them, and that they will only be expected to guess on this game, and learn the words later.

After the guessing session is over, by all means tell the correct

* Roberta Goldstein, Romona School, District No. 39, Wilmette, Illinois.

answer to match each word. The aim is to hold the group's attention through their curiosity about the ones they've missed. Pupils will have to be provided with enough easy words to succeed on so that they'll enjoy the experience.

One example follows of a simple game of this type. It could also be used as a quiz following the unit, and in this way do double duty. Since you want a gay, uninhibited atmosphere, try assigning partners to work together, teaming capable pupils with partners who are less so. Each partnership competes with the other pairs in the class. There are two ways you can operate the game. The first method may be easier to accomplish for the teacher.

Write your words and definitions on a transparency in a scrambled way. Number the words, and letter the definitions. Pass out paper to your teams, and give them instructions to match numbers to the correct letters, using the transparency and one paper to a team.

Another way of doing this might be easier and more fun for the children. Make up a dittomaster with numbered words and lettered definitions, with the words and definitions scrambled so that 1. does not match *a,* etc. Leave triple spaces between each. Run off about 13 copies for a class of 26 children, and use a paper cutter to cut the answers and definitions into small strips. Each pair must receive one of each of the strips, or the equivalent of one dittoed page, so this has to be checked. Then they do their matching on their desks with actual pieces of paper. This gives the children no opportunity to write the incorrect letter by mistake. They can see which definitions are left over, so matching is easier.

Allow enough time so that at least half of your pairs are finished or stumped. Then call time, and read aloud the correct definition for each word, also giving their numbers and letters. The team with the largest number of correctly matched words and definitions will be the winner.

GUESSING GAME

1. antennae
2. spider

a. an animal with six legs and a jointed body
b. a big eye made of sections, including hundreds of eyes—found on houseflies

3. abdomen

4. head

5. thorax

6. wings

7. adult insect

8. eggs

9. drones

10. larvae

11. pupae

12. chrysalis

13. cocoon

14. molting

15. grubs

16. maggots

17. royal jelly

18. exoskeleton

19. compound eye

20. pollen

21. worker bees

22. honeycomb

23. breathing pores

24. nymphs

25. caterpillars

26. glowworms

c. beetle larvae

d. a young insect's way of changing its skin

e. young insects that look like their parents, but cannot fly

f. front part of insect's body, where antennae are

g. the two feelers on an insect

h. an animal with eight legs—not an insect

i. skeleton making up the outside of an insect's body

j. the middle part of an insect's body, where the legs are attached

k. butterfly larvae

l. adult female insects lay these

m. make insects able to fly at some time in their lives

n. larvae of the housefly

o. the largest part of the insect, behind the thorax

p. tiny holes through which insects breathe

q. these young insects hatch from eggs and do not look like their parents

r. the form larvae take when they stop eating, and cover themselves with a shell

s. a moth pupa when it has a silken case

t. female firefly with no wings

u. a butterfly pupa

v. male bees

w. wax city made of thousands of six-sided wax cells

x. female bees who do all the work

y. yellow dust you find in flowers

z. bee milk produced by workers to feed young bee larvae

KEY

1. g.	7. a.	13. s.	20. y.
2. h.	8. l.	14. d.	21. x.
3. o.	9. v.	15. c.	22. w.
4. f.	10. q.	16. n.	23. p.
5. j.	11. r.	17. z.	24. e.
6. m.	12. u.	18. i.	25. k.
		19. b.	26. t.

During the process of checking and figuring the winner, the teacher hopes that the group will become slightly familiar with the unit's science vocabulary. This will not show up as pat definitions that each child will give by rote, but rather as an attitude of increased interest toward the new words, providing more ease in learning this vocabulary later.

DRAW A TREE TO TEACH ROOT WORDS

Even if you cannot draw well, attempt a line drawing of a tree for this next exercise, which is useful from third grade up. The children will not mind a simple sketch, so don't think you need artistic skill to do it. If you prefer not to draw the tree, cut out a picture of a tree and add a sketch of its roots to show it completely. You may wish to draw your sketch before class, using a transparency or a chalkboard.

Choose a simple word like *pay*. Write it near a large root on the tree. Discuss the function of a root to a tree, emphasizing that it is basic to all parts of it. Don't allow anyone to change the subject to food and water for the tree at this point. Agree that the roots provide this, and that they're important, and go on to the rest of the tree.

Point to the trunk, and then the branches of your picture. Ask someone to tell you a word that comes from the root word *pay*. In case no one knows one, give a hint that by adding a prefix or suffix you can make a new word from *pay*. By then you'll have many volunteers. Wait until you get most of the following words from the pupils themselves before you add words of your own. Write each one near a picture of a branch, underlining the prefix and suffix. If you use colored chalk for this, with one color for prefixes and a different hue for suffixes, it will be more interesting to watch.

underpays	prepay	payable	overpayment
underpaid	paying	repayable	payroll
underpayment	repay	prepayable	paymasters
overpay	payment	payments	overpaying
underpay	paid	repayments	payrolls
overpays	repaying	prepayment	pays
overpaid	repayment	paydirt	paymaster
underpaying	prepaid	repays	unpaid
repaid	prepays		

By now you've long run out of branches, so write the rest of your words that you created from *pay* in a list. You've made your point.

If time and interest allow, use this as a chance to have the class tell you what some of the main prefixes and suffixes mean. Show in writing how you're building on *pay* and changing its meaning.

The following words are suggested for similar exercises. Some may be used orally, and others written. Be sure to discuss meanings as you go along.

fun	please	read	change
joy	sad	build	care

For a final exercise, make a dittomaster like the following. Its purpose is review, and to find out whether the children can be tricked by words which seem to, but do not, contain root words and affixes. Pupils should understand by this time that the physical similarity of the letters is not enough to make part of a word into a root word. This part must be related in meaning, or else it is just chance that the letters are familiar. It might be advisable to remind children of the fact that root words are often changed in spelling when prefixes are attached. After this exercise is completed, check it and discuss it together.

FIND THE ROOT WORDS

You will find 25 words below. Many of them contain root words, but some do not, as they are root words themselves. Find and circle all the root words you can. A sample word is done for you. It happens to contain a root word.   SAMPLE: sixty

1. displease
2. sewing
3. fancy
4. changing
5. funny
6. drives
7. joyous
8. butcher
9. going
10. golden
11. beard
12. bearded
13. repaying
14. sadness
15. unhappy
16. regret
17. renew
18. pleasant
19. harpist
20. candle
21. unlighted
22. literature
23. cares
24. carry
25. cars

WORD PARTS

You can help your pupils to read independently by teaching the word parts that are common to many words. First, read the easy word aloud and have children listen for the sounds. Then say the word part, and follow it with the difficult word, saying it by syllables. Children can discover the syllable in the hard word that matches the word part. This lesson can be taught in sections, projected from a visual. Select some of the words most suitable for your grade level.

WORD PARTS

1. w*ish*	ish	accompl*ish*	6. con*test*	est	*est*imate
2. c*oi*n	oi	av*oi*d	7. m*ay*	ay	b*ay*berry
3. b*oy*	oy	emplo*yer*	8. m*ade*	ade	lemon*ade*
4. *pro*gram	pro	*pro*cession	9. curi*ous*	ous	mysteri*ous*
5. s*en*d	en	evid*ent*	10. r*ain*	ain	acqu*ain*ted

CHECKLIST

Enjoy words and the fascinating things you can do with them.

Look for puns that come naturally, and use them unashamedly.

Use words of sincere praise for effort or achievement.

Seek the varied origins of many words and names to give a breadth and sense of history to our language.

Use words, and any trickery you can think of to add to their charm, in order to inflame the imagination of your pupils, and to enhance social studies learning and attitudes.

Try word games to increase and enrich vocabulary and as spelling practice.

Encourage the use of word games for parties, leisure time, and travel pastimes.

Stimulate children to think creatively of words with a game that has words written in a special form to match their meaning.

Share this word game with other classes or with the entire school by featuring it on a bulletin board, and by inviting other children to participate.

Practice quick thinking and vocabulary with *Catalogs,* in which you set a very short time limit within which to think of objects in the room beginning with a specified letter.

Enrich vocabularies with a rhyming game in which two rhyming words match the meaning of something familiar.

Use or compose vocabulary games to fit your science units as introductory activities.

Encourage a relaxed, worry-free attitude toward your new science activity by pairing children for this game, and by letting them know that it's a guessing game on words which they will learn later.

Assume that pupils are totally unfamiliar with the new science vocabulary in your game, and plan some very easy, known, extra words in order to increase the children's enjoyment.

Unlock language meaning with the key of root words.

Use sketches, pictures, and exercises to give understanding and practice in using root words, prefixes, and suffixes.

10

Combined Individualized and Group Spelling Program

You undoubtedly know many people who admit that they cannot spell, and who don't seem to mind it one bit. Let's hope they have dictionary habits or good secretaries. The great differences among individuals in aptitude for spelling do not mean you should throw your hands in the air over the pupils who must struggle to memorize the configuration of each word they write. Neither should you pin roses on those who find it no effort to get perfect spelling papers. These lucky children must have their energies channelled in other directions. You may be wasting a great deal of their time on words they can already spell easily. Find some challenging work for them too.

Most spelling textbooks suggest some simple spelling rules to help the children. Use some of the rules if you wish, but remember that they're hard to learn, easy to forget, and, because of the exceptions, not too effective. Ask yourself how many you remembered. Perhaps you learned a rhyme which stayed with you. That may be something useful to teach:

> Write *i* before *e* except after *c*,
> And when sounded as *a* in *neighbor* and *weigh*.

It's a shame to spoil the rhyme (and the rule), but we should mention these exceptions too: seize weird neither either leisure inveigle.

You'll get an answer to the question of whether we need a weekly word list, and whether it is enough. A method of combining a group lesson approach with individualization will be presented, plus suggestions on where to find the words for individualization. The merits of using phonetics in teaching spelling will be analyzed, and a simple, fairly quiet way to give individual spelling tests will be suggested. You'll read descriptions of spelldowns with new methods, some good spelling games, and a kinesthetic method for helping slow learners in spelling. One school official tells how his district developed a spelling/writing project, with its own specially developed word list, based on the findings of recent research.

Do We Need a Weekly Word List?
Textbook Lists

Many spelling textbooks are attempting to bridge the large gap we find in spelling abilities with the spelling pretest early in the week, to eliminate monotonous rote learning of words already known. Most texts follow the pattern of introducing a weekly word list or unit on Monday. The second day the words are used in sentences. Usually, by Wednesday, what is *called* a pretest is given, and only the words which were not passed on this need to be studied for a final test. Enrichment spelling practice exercises are often supplied for Thursday's work, and methods vary on how pupils are tested on their remaining unpassed words. Our big question is, "Do we *need* a weekly word list?" Very few seem willing to answer it. We all know that children must be taught to spell. Most will agree that a word list is a fairly good system for each week's work. Where all the agreement falls apart is on the question, "What words?"

The use of a textbook series has some real values. We eliminate yearly repetition of the same words by having graded word lists for each school year, with lists getting consecutively harder. This can be a big advantage, especially to an inexperienced teacher who may not know how difficult to make her spelling word lists. There are other values related to various language skills, as practice of the new words on the first day of the week can be a handwriting exercise at the same time pupils learn new words. On Tuesday, the words used in sentences are usually more than a spelling drill, as children learn usage, vocabulary, and practice spelling and handwriting. The main criterion for a good textbook exercise of this type is that it gives clear directions, training pupils for independent work.

Many different word lists from various texts, or a spelling list completely divorced from a textbook, could be good if the teacher knew what words her pupils really needed to learn, so she could make her own lists.

Multi-grade System

A very fine multi-grade system for group teaching was created by one third-grade teacher, and has been adopted by her entire grade level.* She dittoes up a weekly word list, using words from a graded spelling series which teaches one special skill each week at each level.† The weekly list begins with words at a second-grade level, and they progress in difficulty up to sixth-grade work. Each week one special type of word is featured, following the phonics program used in teaching reading. One week there will be short vowels; another week will teach spelling words with long vowels, or words ending with a silent *e*.

The word list can be used in different ways. One teacher uses a long pretest beginning with the second-grade words. She has prepared the children to end their test when the words become too difficult, and they are ready with desk books for when they turn in their tests. A separate test is given for a top group, using the most difficult words on the list. Children practice only the words they have missed. On Friday morning they team up with partners and test each other on individual words. Another teacher uses this same approach, supplementing it with words from the children's work. All of the individual words are kept in a notebook, are practiced individually, and are tested by a partner or by the teacher.

We still haven't answered the original question, however, of whether we *need* the weekly word list. Many districts must think so, as they regularly supply their teachers with spelling texts. I will venture the opinion that we definitely need *some* good weekly word lists. No one has proved which words should be taught at a certain level. Our language contains too many words to teach, so we must concentrate on commonly used words. The textbook spelling lessons are useful for the graded lists and exercises, and in other language areas, so they are worth using if the children can work on their own.

* Margo Turner, Romona School, District 39, Wilmette, Illinois.

† William Kottmeyer and Kay Ware, *Basic Goals in Spelling*, Book 4, (Manchester, Mo.: Webster Division, McGraw-Hill Book Co. 1964).

On Your Own

If you do decide to plan your spelling lessons without a textbook, try to give regular spelling practice using a list of your own. You can use frequently missed words from writing papers, vocabulary words from your reading series, and some words which you may find common to most of the spelling series you look at for your grade level. Words can be grouped in a list according to a central idea or meaning. Another good method groups spelling words by families, such as those with similar endings or digraphs. It will not be enough to count on words from each child's writing papers, since some children never miss words, and a few never try any new ones.

Is the Weekly Word List Enough?

If you wish to continue using your spelling textbook, or to search for one that is more self-directing, we come to another, more vital question, still unasked. "Is the weekly word list enough?" The answer is undoubtedly "No." No matter how skillfully the textbook publisher chooses the graded word lists from typical vocabularies, he cannot provide the words needed for daily use by each individual. Weekly textbook spelling lessons can be supplemented with an individualized approach which will not take much time at all.

WHERE DO WE FIND WORDS FOR INDIVIDUALIZATION?

Pupils' Writing

You've probably guessed by now that the circled words in the proofreading lessons mentioned in Chapter Eight could be used in individual spelling lists. Any system which works for you and the child to signal a new spelling word for his own list may be used. A suggested one is to write *Sp.* near each new word at your proofreading conference. Have the child write in a small spelling notebook all of the new words which he has corrected after they were circled, and help him with words he cannot find in the dictionary. This list will serve as the basis for his own spelling work. A child who missed no words on his writing may have an empty page in his spelling notebook. The teacher should see to it that the unfortunate one who always has a long list gets help, for instance, by giving him frequent opportunities to pass these words.

Missed Pretest Words

This is not all. You have another source of words for each child's individual spelling word list: the weekly spelling test words that were missed on the pretest. The only way to retest words missed on this test without boring the entire class with words they've already passed, is to individualize the missed words by placing them on individual lists. To do this, have the children mark their own spelling word pretest, and list under *Sp.* all the missed words, corrected so that they are accurately spelled. Pupils should not transcribe any words into their own notebooks until you've checked their marking and their lists. It's especially necessary to do this with third- and fourth-graders to prevent them from practicing a word spelled incorrectly.

You will still have a lucky few pupils who seldom miss a word. You can surely provide them with other responsibilities on the day that each child is required to practice his own spelling words.

Procedure

Pretest

The most logical way to teach spelling using a textbook or other word list would be to give a group pretest on Monday, using the weekly list, *before* practicing the new words. Mark it together right after the pretest.

Practice and Enrichment

Use the textbook sentence exercises on the second day according to their value. If they teach other language skills, as many do, and if children can work independently with them, the activity may be worthwhile for this alone. If the textbook exercise has no value other than as spelling practice, your class could spend its time better on other things. This is especially true of the children who already know the words. You may want to assign these exercises to the few who really need them. Supervise the entering of missed pretest words on individual lists. Allow time on Wednesday for practice on individual lists, using word practice or sentences, after demonstrating the study method, using a new word. Give the children who pass their pretest words and have none on their own list, something better to do than practice words they already know. Allow each child to study only the words that were missed.

Study Method

1. *Look* at the word carefully.
2. *Say* the word slowly.
3. *Think* about the word. How does it start? What sounds do you hear? Do you hear any vowels? Does one vowel say its own name? Is there a silent vowel? Is there a silent consonant? Does the word have two parts, or syllables, to study?
4. *Write* the word and look at it. Did you spell it correctly?
5. *Practice* writing the word at least five times, saying it softly as you write it.

Provide Bonus Words,—difficult words given for extra credit.

The final Friday test would be individualized on each child's own spelling list, as some will have a few words, all different, and many will have none. If you use a few helpers to give the individual tests with you before and after class, and during spare moments, the testing will be done very quietly, but too slowly. Allow children to test each other as partners on Friday morning. They can do the job quickly and well if you pair them with forethought. Two children with long lists would not make a good team, nor would two children with no words at all. Be on hand to help your slow readers, and see that the tests they have to give are not too long.

Progress Charts

If you use the Monday pretest, plus the individual method, you will probably not want the textbook progress chart filled out, as your class's textbook words are group tested before they're studied. If you want a progress chart, devise a simple system at the top of each individual notebook page. The first entry could be a number of words to pass for the week. The second could be the number of these words which were passed. It should not be a competitive chart, but would keep a personal record for each child.

By using the group plus the individual approach in spelling words, you get the advantage of a list of words graded in difficulty, which most children of a certain age should know, plus words actually *used* by pupils. Words children regularly miss, words they use all of the time to express themselves in writing, surely must constitute the backbone of their lists. The combination of the two approaches will give you a balanced spelling program which meets individual needs. The one who needs it most works the hardest in spelling. The others will be assigned tasks in different curriculum areas which *they* need.

CAN PHONETICS HELP SPELLING?

Helps

Yes, of course it can, with some conditions. We cannot spell a word correctly until we hear it well. Many words can be spelled by just sounding them out, and a large part of the common spelling errors could be remedied by this. A child may miss an entire syllable in his spelling due to being in a hurry, or to careless habits. Each letter in a word should be sounded carefully as a spelling word is checked.

Limitations

The limitations of the phonetic approach include both the expected and unexpected. Unexpected ones are the limits set by children with speech problems. Children who do not pronounce their *r's* may leave them out or change them in their spelling. One little boy had a speech impediment caused by a severe nasal allergy. His nose was always stuffed, and he spelled his words the way they sounded to him. He agreed that a word sounded differently when others said it, but he said it in a stuffed up way more often, so it became a habit. The expected limits are the many words in our language which do not get spelled the way they sound. The following list could be endless, but a few examples are given:

weigh	plague	lamb	fasten	write	tough
neighbor	through	teach	break	graph	

Another limitation on the usefulness of phonetics is regional variation in accent, causing some letters to be eliminated entirely. So, phonetics must be used to help in spelling whenever possible by clearly sounding out each sound and syllable in regularly spelled words. For the many exceptions which must be memorized, try to find patterns, so groups of similar words can be learned together. They won't seem so formidable that way.

EVERYONE LOVES A BONUS

A complete spelling program always offers something so very challenging that it seems ridiculously impossible. Plan on a Bonus Word list each week for stimulation. It will keep the lucky ones with spelling aptitude on their toes. However, a good Bonus Word list must be geared for each child in the class, as everyone must feel free to earn a bonus. Devise a group of words ranging in difficulty from the very easy to the almost impossible. Try to include a few words from your current events discussions, names of continents, tongue-twisters, and a few words of the type that are regularly missed all through high school, such as *their* and *there*. Use words from social studies and science units, and take time to discuss the meanings of the Bonus Words. For words like *their* and *there* to have any value when practiced, place a signal word after them, or a little sketch. For example, write them this way:

their house	or	their	
over there	or	there	
which (?)		witch	

You may be wondering how you can give a bonus if these words are passed. One way is for each child to begin, early in the school year, an extra credit notebook containing a page for each subject. On the spelling page each Bonus Word will receive one check mark, with special words earning higher values. Pupils need reminding to write their check marks in as they're earned. If pupils keep extra credit pages, follow through monthly by collecting notebooks in order to check and encourage progress.

Allow some free time on the day you present the Bonus Words. Have paper available, and encourage everyone to try at least one or two. If a child does not choose to practice these words, allow him this freedom, as he will be more likely to want to do it the next week if he has a free choice. Make a point of it that no person will be tested, or can earn a bonus, on a word that he hasn't practiced five times. This may sound like a lot of bookkeeping work to you, but a record can be kept easily of individual Bonus Words practiced by using a dittoed class list. Jot down the one or two words practiced by some individuals after their names on the class list. In the case of the ambitious few who practice the entire list, just write *all* after their names. Then, when it is time to test children on their own Bonus Words, you don't waste energy by giving pupils words they probably don't know. You can check the Bonus Word tests and hand them back for entering on extra credit pages. Children enjoy this type of test, so by giving Bonus Words with a wide range of difficulty, even the timid children will try for a bonus, which is very encouraging to them.

26 TEST HELPERS—THEY LEARN AS THEY TEST

If you've never tried individual testing, you may say to yourself that it would be great, if it wasn't impossible. If you try to do it yourself it's not impossible, but it is time-consuming, and your conference time with some children could be better spent on phonics or some special need. How to solve the problem? Look around you at 26 or more eager helpers. They would much rather stop whatever they are doing right now (unless it's recess time), and give a spelling test to another pupil. Many would even miss recess to do this. Would it be bedlam with 13 or more little voices giving oral spelling words, plus sentences? With careful planning, it works very well, and is only slightly noisy. In case you're not ready to attempt this, try a planned helper system. Assign two helpers each month, giving everyone a chance by the end of the year. Select mature pupils at first, and give the few who are not able to assume responsibility a chance to grow up a bit. Spend some time supervising your helpers as they give their first few spelling tests, to make sure that names are on each test, that they pronounce words correctly, that they give good, clear sentences, and that they give no help other than repeating the words. Once your helpers know how to test, you will be impressed by their efficiency. Set limits as to when testing is to be conducted. Before and after class, during routine writing periods, and when the helpers' work is finished, are good times. Insure a respect for reading time by enforcing absolute quiet and no testing at that time. Once you see how much help pupils can be, you'll find other tasks for them too. One fine aspect of helper testing is that your helpers are practicing spelling as they give the tests and help you.

The words for individual testing will be written on a class list by the teacher, as the words are written on the pupils' papers for entry in their notebooks. At testing time the master class list can be cut into strips for testing.

A SPELLING/WRITING PROJECT BECOMES AN ENGLISH PROGRAM

A brave new plan, based on much research, being used in the Glenview, Illinois Public Schools, began as a Spelling/Writing Project, and has since developed into a total English program, which is going well.* This plan has been written up by Glenview's Assistant Superintendent of Schools, Robert L. Hillerich. Parts of his article, reporting from these schools, are reproduced here:

> Few areas of the elementary school curriculum receive more comment with less result than does the teaching of spelling. In the Glenview schools we were determined to follow discussion with action, but our concern was a dual one. We wanted children to learn to spell correctly rather than phonetically, but more so we wanted them to become more fluent in written language. Our children, as we saw them year after year, were above average in ability, could talk on many subjects easily, read well, misspelled phonetically, and generally resisted the discipline of putting their thoughts on paper.
>
> Research has pretty thoroughly undermined the typical commercial approach to spelling. For example, it appears that correctness in spelling is as much a matter of attitude and interest as it is a skill. Goss found that children actually knew how to spell fifty percent of the words they misspelled in their written compositions.† The assumed reason for the misspelling of half of these words must relate to attitudes—the children were careless, in a hurry, or did not go back to proofread what they had written.
>
> What are we doing in our schools to further the proper attitude that is so necessary if we expect children to be correct spellers? Are we developing this attitude by putting children through the typical five-day-a-week spelling program? Are we

* Robert L. Hillerich, "A Spelling/Writing Project Becomes an English Program," *Illinois ASCD Newsletter of Curriculum and Supervision*, Illinois Association for Supervision and Curriculum Devpt., Springfield, Ill., Vol. 14, No. 2, March, 1968, pp. 1-3.

† James Goss, "Analysis of Accuracy of Spelling in Written Compositions of Elementary School Children and the Effects of Proofreading upon Accuracy", Ed.D dissertation, Norman: Univ. of Oklahoma, 1959.

fostering this attitude by having children study lists of words, seventy-five percent of which they know before they have begun to study them? Are we fostering this attitude, or even developing any skill in spelling, by having children fill in contextual blanks, study rules about spelling, or do phonic exercises to practice these rules?

Research and experience would suggest that we are wasting much of children's time in these activities that are included in a typical spelling program. As stated by Horn and many others, we should spend no more than one hour per week on spelling.* We can do this if we eliminate many of the time-wasting activities that are so prevalent. For example, time is saved and spelling is taught more effectively if words are presented in list form rather than in context.†

One of the most agreed upon findings of research is the value of a pretest.‡ A pretest with immediate correction by the child will determine which words can be eliminated and which words need to be studied. While the teacher's stressing of hard spots in words is of no value to children—because each child has his own hard spot—the immediate correction of a pretest will help each youngster to identify his own personal hard spots in words, the points on which he needs to put emphasis.

Commercial spelling programs do take advantage of a few points indicated by the research. They usually provide some means whereby the child can keep a record of his progress in spelling. They do emphasize, or at least provide for emphasis of, the study method in spelling, and this in turn usually calls for attention to visual imagery and visual discrimination, both of which have been found to be important factors in learning to spell. Further than that, as pointed out in a summary of the research by Dorothy Bredin, traditional spelling programs are not justified and have little foundation in research findings.§

A basic tenet of most commercial programs is that a generalization approach, that is, a building of spelling power, is an important method in teaching spelling. Yet the research suggests

---

*Ernest Horn, "Spelling," *Encyclopedia of Educational Research,* New York: Macmillan, 1960.

†Thomas D. Horn, "Research in Spelling," *Elementary English,* March, 1960, pp. 174-177.

‡Thomas D. Horn, "The Effect of the Corrected Test on Learning To Spell," *Elementary School Journal,* Jan., 1947, pp. 277-285.

§Dorothy M. Bredin, "Is the Present Typical Commercial Approach to Spelling in Grades Two Through Six Justified by Research?", Master's Paper, Evanston: National College, March, 1966.

the reverse: children learn to spell the words that they study specifically for spelling.† In fact, in the computer study done at Stanford, Paul Hanna reported that, while 84 percent of the 17,000 words examined were consistently spelled when they were put into the computer phoneme by phoneme, the same 17,000 words were only 49 percent consistent when they were analyzed as whole words.‡ When we consider that children must spell *whole words* correctly or incorrectly and that the computer was programmed for many more rules than any child can be programmed for, even the 49 percent is probably an exaggerated estimate of our ability to teach children to spell correctly through rules.

What has been said thus far and what is implied by the research is that spelling can probably best be taught strictly from a word list with a pretest for each week's words before the children begin studying. This pretest, with immediate correction by the child, should be followed by review of the study method as needed and by application of the study method to the words that were missed on the pretest. A retest on Wednesday of the words missed and a retest on Friday could comprise the entire spelling program.

Such an approach was piloted in the Glenview Schools in 1964, using experimental and control groups with a pre- and post-test design. Results indicated that children in the experimental program scored as well on the test of studied words as did children in the control group who used a commercial program, and that children in the experimental program scored significantly better on unstudied words, despite the fact that the control group supposedly was building spelling power. The experimental group was studying twice as many words per week as the control group but was devoting only three days a week to spelling, as compared with the five days a week given to spelling in the commercial program.

What happened in the two periods each week that were stolen from the traditional spelling program? This probably is the crucial point in the entire program. Those two periods were devoted to additional experiences in written language: writing, revising, and the teaching of proofreading skills. Teachers reported a great increase in interest in spelling correctly. What with the crowded

---

† Walter Petty, "Phonetic Elements as Factors in Spelling Difficulties," *Journal of Educational Research*, November, 1957, pp. 209-214.

‡ Paul Hanna et al, "Phoneme-Grapheme Correspondences as Cues to Spelling Improvement," Washington: Government Printing Office, 1966.

school day, children were able to do at least twice as much in the way of written language as they had done in the past because of the two added periods. Such an approach puts spelling into proper perspective. There is no point in learning to spell orally, and there is no point in learning to spell words that one is not going to use in his writing.

This truism leads us, however, to a problem. What words should children study in spelling if we take a word list approach? The obvious answer would be the words that they will use in writing. A priority should be placed on the most frequently used words being taught first, but where does one find such a list? Commercial spellers are of no value as a source for words to be taught. Wise compared twenty spelling programs and found very little agreement as to words taught or the grade level at which these words should be taught.* In a comparison of sixteen commercial spelling programs from second through sixth grade, Hillerich found only 486 words common to the sixteen programs, even when grade placement was ignored.† Considering grade level placement, only forty words were agreed upon by the sixteen programs and these were all in second grade. Not only that, some very peculiar placements of words arose: for example, the words *with* and *out* were unanimously placed at grade two, but the compound *without* ranged from grade two to grade five; twenty-nine words spanned the grades, from two to six. While an average of 2,167 words was taught by sixth grade, a total of 5,327 words was included in the sixteen programs.

With so little agreement among commercial spelling books, one might go to the basic word lists such as Thorndike or Rinsland. Here, however, problems arise in that the word lists are very badly dated.

In order to develop a current word list, the Glenview Schools, in 1966, engaged in a frequency count involving over a third of a million running words from children's creative writing in grades two through six. That word list is being used as part of the spelling program described above. Teachers, during the school year 1966-1967, kept a tally of words missed by children so that an estimate of the difficulty of each word could be established. The word lists are now balanced in terms of difficulty as well as frequency.

---

* Carl T. Wise, "Selections and Gradation of Words in Spelling," *Elementary School Journal*, June, 1934, pp. 754-766.

† Robert L. Hillerich, "A Comparison of Word Lists in Sixteen Commercial Spelling Programs," unpublished study, 1965.

An interesting sidelight of the word count is the additional evidence it offers that existing word lists are certainly outdated. For example, we found that Fitzgerald's 2,650 word spelling vocabulary has many words that are not used at all by children today.* Twenty-five percent of Horn's First Hundred Words were not among the first hundred most frequently used by Glenview children.

A somewhat shocking discovery came from this study of the words used by children in grades two through six in their written language: only 10,446 different words were used throughout the grades in this third of a million words. When derivatives of basic words were eliminated, the number of different root words was less than 6,000. When one considers that Rinsland reported 11,304 different words used at sixth grade in 1937, a question arises.† This question again is related to children's attitudes toward spelling. Are we, in our emphasis on correct spelling, leading children to use more basic—and often less appropriate—words in their writing merely because these are the words they know how to spell? Can we get spelling back into proper perspective by putting our emphasis on the expression of thoughts, on the communication of ideas in writing in the clearest and most interesting manner possible? To do this, we must place spelling, along with the various mechanics of punctuation and capitalization, in the proper frame of reference as one aspect of revision and proofreading.

Once the teaching of spelling was established in our schools, the desire to improve written language—far stronger than any concern about spelling per se—motivated the staff to further exploration.

SPELLDOWNS AREN'T OLD HAT— WITH THESE NEW TRIMMINGS

Finding Time

Everybody loves a spelldown—even the pupils. Not every teacher finds the time for them, but anyone you'll ask will wistfully reminisce about the wonderful spelldowns of his childhood. The school day

---

* James A. Fitzgerald, *A Basic Life Spelling Vocabulary*, Milwaukee: Bruce Publishing Company, 1951.

† Henry D. Rinsland, *A Basic Vocabulary of Elementary School Children*, New York: Macmillan, 1945.

just seems too full to allow time for spelldowns. A way to squeeze one in and not rush it is to persuade your class to vote for a spelldown for an indoor recess activity. They think they're getting an extra long recess when you extend the spelldown. It works once in a while.

Oral or Written?

There are two main ways to conduct a spelldown. They are alike in these points: you divide the class into two equal teams standing on opposite sides of the room, and teams alternate turns trying to get as many words spelled correctly as possible. If a word is missed, the pupil sits down, and he's out of the game. At the end of the spelldown there are just a few pupils on each side competing with each other. Declare the first team to go below three members as the loser, as the last two can go on and on. If your time is up and you must decide on a winner before you narrow the game down this far, call the team with the most players still standing the winner. The original method of giving the word orally, repeating it in a sentence, and saying it a third time is still used. One way of playing has the team member spelling the word orally, and this is still done by a few. A newer, *much* better, method is for the pupil to write the word on a chalkboard or on the overhead projector. Educators feel that the group as a whole will benefit more from the spelled word by seeing it written correctly, than by hearing it spelled aloud. If the word should be written incorrectly, the teacher says, "Sorry, incorrect," and the pupil erases it quickly and sits down. The player from the other team must try to spell this same word, but he has the advantage of having seen which way was incorrect. This should keep everyone watching closely. There are no scores to keep, and the only rules should be strict silence, with penalties for laughing, loud coughing, or other signals to help a team member; and a time limit. A reasonable time should be given each child to write his word. If you allow too long a time the game becomes tedious and loses its excitement. The signal that a child is through with the word can be his setting down his chalk.

There are many special days when the children are too restless to do any written work requiring intense concentration. For instance, before or after a special music program or field trip, or when the weather is very hot and humid. A spelldown will be a welcome activity to everyone, and can be valuable spelling practice. If you have a small portable chalkboard, and a quiet, shaded corner of your playground, an outdoor spelldown can be a delightful way to end a hot afternoon. Be sure to bring erasers, extra chalk, and to explain rules and conduct expected.

SPELLING GAMES

Mapdown

Try a game called Mapdown for third grade and up. It will help teach not only spelling, but map skills as well. While competitive in nature, it should be conducted in a spirit of teamwork and fun. Let's assume that the class is reviewing the study of North America in front of a large map. Have a pointer handy, and divide the group into two even teams. The teacher conducts the game and functions as timekeeper. Allow enough time in order to accomplish something worthwhile. To play the game the teacher calls out a place name, beginning with those most familiar, and getting progressively into the more difficult ones. The first pupil in line would spell the name of the place, writing it on the chalkboard before pulling down the map, and he would then use the pointer to locate the place on the map. Try a one-minute time limit, during which the child must locate and point to the place or go down. Allow a point for correct spelling, with capital letter, and a point for finding the place on the map. Teams would alternate, pulling the map up again between turns. Try to use locations which are important in human geography, instead of obscure mountains and lakes. The last pupil standing would win for his team, and could earn ten extra credits (five for each) in social studies and science. Give six extra credits to each other member of the winning team, dividing them between the two subjects. Try to keep the place names reasonably easy to spell. The Okefenokee Swamp would not be fair; nor would it be an especially useful word to children anywhere but Florida or Georgia.

Macaroni Spelling

This game will take quite a large supply of alphabet macaroni. Place a pile to macaroni on each desk, and at a signal from you, pupils spell out a verse from some poem you'd like them to become familiar with. Project the poem on the lightboard in case you do not have one for each child in your English books or readers. Place extra piles of letters at about eight locations about the room, for people who may be missing certain letters. If they all go to the same place, the game takes on a slightly different character. At a given time, if no one has finished, select as winner the child who has correctly completed the most. Prevent pupils from eating the raw macaroni by stressing how dirty it is from handling. Vary regular spelling practice by using macaroni to spell out the words.

Spelling Can Be Rough—Try Sandpaper

There are always a few children who do not learn all of the spelling words, and who forget the words they do learn very quickly. Written and oral drills have been tried, plus written exercises, testing, practice, retesting, and games, and these pupils are still spelling poorly. How can we help them? We've used our entire bag of tricks, plus much individual help and encouragment. However, children do not all learn in the same way. The usual methods of teaching reach the child through the senses of sight and hearing. Try the sense of touch, which will be useful in teaching handwriting too. The teacher can work with this tactile method in helping individuals to learn spelling words and patterns.

Preparing the Letters

The preparation for this special help takes time, but when you prepare a set of rough sandpaper manuscript letters you can use them for years. These sandpaper forms can also be used in practicing the letters of manuscript writing for young children who are learning to write, or who write them incorrectly. To make your set of letters, select certain heights for small, middle, and large letters, and be consistent. A three-inch letter is ideal, but a two-inch letter will do very well. Measure and draw your letters on the back of the sandpaper. Since the letters will have to be drawn backwards it will be easiest if you have a cardboard form which you can turn over. Once the prepared letters are drawn on the sandpaper, cut them out with scissors, or use a razor blade in a holder, on a wooden board. Glue letters on tagboard.

Kinesthetic Practice

Teach one or a few children to use these rough letters by demonstrating. Trace the shape of each letter with the tip of your right forefinger, reversing this if you are left-handed. Trace with the same motions you would use in writing the letter, saying its name aloud. Do this with a complete word and then have the child repeat your procedure, so he gets the full benefit from the rough texture. This is not a magic formula, but it may help some and it will also break the monotony of practicing in the same way for those who have to practice so often.

Other Practice Methods

Norelco produces a tape-recording cassett that snaps into a portable battery-powered tape recorder, and a headset with attached microphone.* The tape has a non-erasable master track containing the teacher's lesson, prerecorded with pauses between phrases. The student repeats the phrases, then listens and compares himself with the teacher. He can then record and compare again. This can be

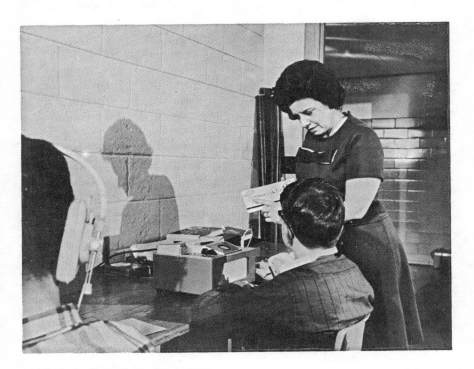

Figure 10-1. The Bell & Howell Language Master,® an audio-visual instructional system, is one modern teaching aid receiving widespread use in education today.

---

* Norelco LCH 1000, Norelco Training and Education, North American Philips Co., Inc., Dept. NJ-1, 100 E. 42nd St., New York, N. Y., 10017.

used independently for any kind of repetitive work. It will be even more valuable in spelling if the pupil has a list to look at as he hears the words spelled.

A versatile audiovisual machine that has unlimited prossibilities for language arts use is the Bell & Howell Language Master ® Audio-Visual Instructional System.† Pre-printed and pre-recorded cards, as well as blank cards, are available, with lengths of magnetic tape adhered parallel to their bottom edges. This feature allows the Language Master unit to function as a dual-channel audio recorder and playback device. Headphones and jack are provided. The pre-recorded and pre-printed cards tie the audio with the visual, and their use can be extended with realia, leading to tactile, olfactory, and tasting experiences, with applications for handicapped learners too.

CHECKLIST

Use a weekly word list, giving a pretest before the new words are studied.

Collect words from reading textbooks, children's writing, and various spelling series, if you decide to devise your own word lists.

Individualize spelling practice and instruction by having each child collect missed words from his daily papers, plus corrected words from his textbook pretest, for his own spelling notebook list.

Keep spelling rules few, short, simple, and rhymed, if possible.

Provide challenging activities in other subjects during spelling practice time for good spellers who finish quickly.

Use phonetics as a *limited* help in correctly hearing spelling words, considering irregular spellings, variations in speech and accent, and speech or nasal handicaps.

Make use of as many research findings as possible.

Provide some means for the child to keep records of his progress.

Emphasize the study method in practice.

Encourage spelling practice and growth by using Bonus Words each week, ranging from the easy to the very challenging.

Expect Bonus Words to be practiced before testing by helpers is allowed.

Use partners to give weekly individual spelling tests to each other.

---

† Bell & Howell Co., 7100 McCormick Rd., Chicago, Ill. 60645.

Train two helpers each month to give individual spelling tests and Bonus Word tests before and after class, or in their spare time.

Improve on the good old spelldown by having the spelling word written rather than spelled orally.

Include regular spelling games in your plans, relating them to other subjects if you can.

Help slow spellers patiently and cheerfully with every method you can devise, including the kinesthetic.

11

Motivating and Teaching Techniques to Make Handwriting Fun

Here are some introductory techniques that pinpoint the best letters to teach first and last, as well as specific ideas on how to encourage the extensive practice needed for legible, attractive handwriting. You will learn ways to make the child responsible for his own progress, and an effective means of evaluating it so as to keep the pupil's parents aware of gains and the child stimulated by success. Ways of preventing and correcting bad writing habits are analyzed, and suggestions are given for achieving an efficient balance between group lessons and individualization of instruction.

THE FIRST STEPS IN INTRODUCING CURSIVE WRITING

In teaching cursive writing for the first time, the group lesson can exploit the natural enthusiasm which always accompanies a totally new experience. You will have pupils' attention as you may never have it again, so help them get off to a fine start by stressing good posture, clear desks, and correct hand position. Wide spaced paper is essential, but two narrow spaces can be used as one space divided in half. Show the class how to rule top guide line, as shown in Figure 11-1.

A long, sharp No. 2 pencil is best. It's useful to have extra pencils ready to lend, as it is vital that no short, stubby stumps be used, since they lead to an incorrect grasp. Demonstrate a good, loose grasp of a

Figure 11-1.

pencil by pulling it easily through your fingers. Explain how a tight fist tires the hand and cramps the fingers. You can have a little fun by pretending to be the horrible example with a short pencil and a hand position like a boxer ready to punch. Demonstrate how the blood leaves the fingers and how they get numb.

You can teach paper position to all children, whether right- or left-handed, by showing the paper tilted with its lower corner aimed at the front edge of the desk, pointed at its center. The slant of paper varies with left- or right-handedness, but the point remains the same, in the center. If feet can reach the floor they should be there. Select a few pupils who are sitting straight, with their feet on the floor. When you praise them nearly everyone will straighten up. Hand position is not as easy, as some have formed incorrect habits earlier, and may have a strained grasp with a tight fist. Time, patience, and joking reminders will slowly help this.

To introduce a new letter use a method of tracing it in the air to match the wall chart. The class copies this air tracing. Then write the letter a few times before they try it on paper. This is best done on the overhead projector, but can be effective on a lined chalkboard.

Introduce *a* first as an example of a lower case letter which uses half a space and touches the half space line. The shape and height

Figure 11-2.

of a letter are taught together, so no incorrect habits are formed. An important "first" is the idea of slant, which is a big change from the straight manuscript letter. Some children learn slant so well that they begin to slant their manuscript writing, but you can straighten that out. To begin with slant show a few slanting lines and write a letter over one and near the other.

Too little special attention has been given to the problems of the left-handed child. A left-handed pupil achieves a right slant by placing his hand above the line and bending his wrist to get the pencil on the line. The result is tension, less speed, and smeared writing as the hand rubs work previously written. He should not use this incorrect hand position, but should slant to the left, a backhand slant. The pupil must conform to reading usage by writing from left to right. A left-handed child who has formed a habit of a right slant may find it natural to keep it, but backhand practice can help him to a correct hand position.* Teach the left slant to children who are first learning cursive writing, as a more comfortable grip must lead to more legible handwriting.

The next letter to teach is *l*, as many other tall letters begin with the *l* form. It is the first example of a tall letter, so you should stress that it must touch the dotted line above the half space line, but never the top line. It helps if you give a logical reason for things, so

* Mildred B. Plunkett, *A Writing Manual for Teaching the Left-handed,* 2nd ed., (Cambridge, Mass.: Educators Publishing Service, 1967), p. 1.

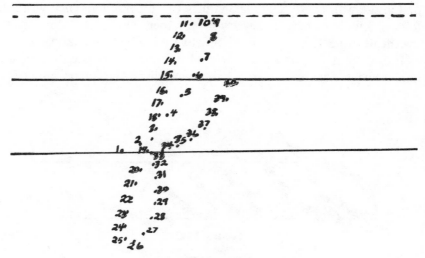

Figure 11-3.

explain that the reason for the space near the top line is to prevent a crowding of letters on adjacent lines, so that your eyes will not get confused.

After *l* it is logical to teach *b, f, h,* and *k,* since they all begin with the *l* form. With a letter like *f* it is good to watch carefully at the start to see that the bottom loop is not being reversed, a common occurrence. One means of achieving this is to prepare a dot-to-dot puzzle sheet, as shown in Figure 11-3. Make it large enough to read the numerals easily. This directs the pupils to begin correctly, and is a pleasant diversion from ordinary practicing.

The letters *m, n, v, x, y,* and *z* are taught together, to show how the start of an *n* is the beginning of all the others. This is illustrated in Figure 11-4. A reminder of slant is very useful with the *z,* as children have a tendency to distort the lower loop by placing it to the right of the letter, rather than following the slant.

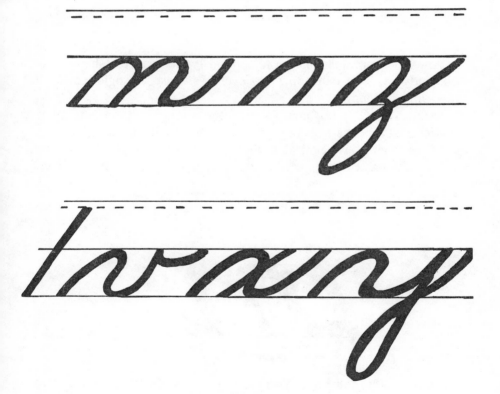

Figure 11-4.

Teach *d, g,* and *q,* by reviewing *a,* which begins the same way.

Study capital, or upper case, letters after all the lower case letters have been introduced. Don't wait until proficiency is achieved, as children like something new, and this gives them a lift. Work on simple joinings as soon as possible, because they lead to words. The difficult joinings must be specifically taught. Don't wait too long with *os* and *wr,* as it is a worry to the child why the *s* doesn't close, and why the *r* doesn't look the same. This is illustrated in Figure 11-5.

Figure 11-5.

Another source of concern to a pupil is the distorted shape of *or, on,* and *om.* You can appeal to a child's sense of logic, as in the following incident.

"Mrs. Ashley," a boy complained, "the *n* in *on* only has one hump. We learned that the *n* has two humps. I'm all mixed up."

"I see what you mean," I replied. "Tom, let's look at it this way. The *n* still has two humps, but the first one is bent a lot so it can

Figure 11-6.

reach the *o.* I'll show you." You can see the bent hump in Figure 11-6.

He didn't answer, but gave a big smile, so this dilemma was resolved. He looked at *om* too, and he was relieved to see that the third hump really *was* there, but was just "bent a lot." This is illustrated in Figure 11-7.

Figure 11-7.

EARN YOUR NAME CARD

The first thing a child really *wants* to write is his own name, so as soon as he is ready for words begin a concentrated drive to perfect each child's first name. Do not wait until there is proficiency in all capital letters, as each pupil must only concentrate on one.

You can begin the year in third grade with manuscript name cards taped to each desk. Laminate them if possible. They are useful in the beginning as you learn their names, and they are a great help to substitute teachers all year. Have ready a full set of name cards with complete names written in cursive writing. After a few days of practice on the first name, when the novelty has worn off, show the brand-new cursive name cards which they've never seen. Pass the cards out for practice work, and collect them later as if they were rare jewels. They are shown as a prize to be worked for, and emphasize that the name cards must be earned. A pupil's objective will be to write his first name well, and when he's ready he asks to try out for it at any time. You are to be the judge.

When a child is doing fairly well on his name point out which letter or joining is keeping him from earning the card, and work on that with him. Be careful to give the card only when the child and you both know he's doing well. It's understood that he will want to write his last name well too, so that is the next project after the prized card is taped on his desk. The cursive card is also handy for reference when he's practicing. Once the first card is awarded it's amazing how hard the other children drive themselves to improve their names. It's easy to check on possible winners who are too modest to try out. When they write their name beautifully on their daily papers it's your cue to award the cursive card. There is, of course, no censure for the slower child who is still struggling for legibility. Sometimes you can use a spare moment to quietly write a slow child's name on his paper as he watches. He copies it as well as he can, and usually replies with a grateful grin for helping him try to win too. Never give a card out to make a child feel good, because he wouldn't get the feeling of accomplishment unless he'd really won it. If it is near the end of the school year there are ways of intensifying practice so that he *finally* writes a good one. You don't wait for him to repeat the triumph at this point. You just award the card, shake his hand, give him the masking tape, and heave a sigh of relief.

USE LINED COLOR TRANSPARENCIES

You can teach handwriting for years without the overhead projector, but you'll have so much fun with it that you can understand the children's delight in using it.

It is a simple matter to draw a line for the half space, and a dotted line for the top guide line a bit below the top line. Use an attractive colored transparency. Once the pencil-lined paper is put through a copying machine the pencil lines are permanent and cannot wash off when a child washes off his practice writing.

You can begin your group lessons as you pass out lined papers with individual assignments on them. To do this jot down a few letters for each child as you check his written work during the week. Use a class list, as it is fast and easy that way. Select the letters which need special work the most, and write these as models on individual papers. Each pupil spends the first ten minutes of the lesson practicing his own special needs. Walk about looking for especially good forms, and when you see one make a note of the person and the letter. When individual practice time is up call on these pupils to

Figure 11-8. "Floating L."

come up to the overhead projector and demonstrate their skill. As a child writes his letter on the lined color transparency there is often critical comment from members of the group; this should be kept in constructive channels. The class learns this way to analyze good points as well as things which need improving.

You may wish to use this vocabulary for handwriting analysis. It is very specific and pupils enjoy it. If a letter does not touch the line call it *floating*. See Figure 11-8.

If a letter falls below the line it is said to be *sinking*. A *sinking l* is shown in Figure 11-9.

Figure 11-9. "Sinking L."

This analysis leads to children wanting to mark their own practice papers. They cross out the *sinking, floating,* and incorrectly formed letters which don't match the models on the color transparency. The signal for a very good letter is to circle it. Try to walk around the room and circle at least one letter for each child if you can. If no letter is correct you can write an easy letter and keep repeating it until it is copied correctly and you can circle it. By emphasizing the good the child learns not to brood over the poor letters he writes, and he gleefully crosses them out himself. When you collect the papers, instead of marking them with letter grades, circle the good letter forms, cross out the poor ones, and write letters as models when the form needs re-introduction.

Besides the models prepared with a special pen on colored transparencies, you can also use a plastic ruler showing models of the upper and lower case alphabets on the overhead projector.

How to Cope With Eager After-School Practicing

Although this might seem to be a complex problem, it is possible to keep three children very happy at the overhead projector. One can write, using a special color pen, and two can watch, awaiting their turns. If a line builds up and everyone is tense, it's easy to find errands for them to run, and also, there are always many chalkboards and ledges to wash. Due to scout meetings, dental appointments, lessons, religious school classes, and suddenly-remembered shopping excursions, the line usually thins out to manageable proportions anyway. You may have had children writing happily at the chalkboard, but until you try the colored transparencies and overhead projector you may never have an after-school line. This kind of practice is superior to that on paper, as you can make suggestions and corrections before bad habits are formed. You can also praise a good letter without stopping any work you may be doing, as it's so easy to watch.

"HOW AM I DOING?"—SELF-EVALUATION

A grade is only one way to evaluate a pupil's performance. Another method is to compare samples of work. This is much better than a mark, because the child himself can compare an early handwriting sample with a later one and see success. The good thing about it is that even a little improvement shows up dramatically.

Ask the class to copy identical samples, and date them October, December, February, and June. The new copy is stapled to the old. The best sample to use is one that contains both lower and upper case letters, including most letters and some difficult joinings. A list of the days of the week and the major holidays is good.

You can send the samples home four times a year so that the pupil can show them off to his parents. By December there is an old copy for comparison. It is sometimes difficult to get them back because the children are so proud of the improvement. You won't have to sell handwriting practice, as the class knows that their next sample must be better than the last. Give plenty of notice before the sample, and if there should be a regression or no progress for one period do not emphasize it. The main goal is improvement from October to June. It's always there, in some degree. Children thrive on achievement, and even a little leads to more of the same.

If, for some reason, a child is reluctant to use cursive writing and make the change from manuscript, it is best not to force it. He may not be ready physically, and since the social pressures for progress are so strong, it is better to encourage rather than demand. By the end of the year most are on their way. In the case of laziness, you may wish to use a system of penalties at the end of the year, taking off points for papers written in manuscript writing. It is necessary to know the child well to decide whether or not to use this. There are some fourth-graders who are not able to write well at the middle of the school year, but these are the rare cases. These children will also gain by comparing their samples. They usually show dramatic changes in muscle control.

WHAT TO DO IF THEY'RE PRACTICING INCORRECTLY

If you notice that a child keeps repeating an incorrect letter form or height, stop the paper practice and have him work where you can watch. The overhead projector is best, but a nearby chalkboard is useful. When the letter form is good, have him practice a few rows at your desk. Take the time to circle good letters so he can repeat them. Be generous with praise when it's truthful. If a child shows fatigue continue at another time. It is good to stop on a happy note rather than one of frustration.

KINESTHETIC METHODS

If repeated practice and teacher's demonstrations do not produce correct letter forms, then a new method is the answer. Some children do not learn well visually, and a new avenue to the senses must be tried. It will give the pupil some variety too, as by this time he may be bored with the repeated practice and resistant to it.

There are two good methods in use. Both ways use the kinesthetic sense, the sense of touch.

One method uses letters cut from the roughest textured sandpaper you can find. The Art Department often has it. The child traces the sandpaper letter exactly as it would be written, using his index finger.

The other method uses a flat pan of clay or similarly plastic material. The letters are carved in the clay with a stick, and the resulting depressions can be traced with the fingers.*

---

* Reva White, Learning Disabilities Specialist, Central and Romona Schools, District No. 39, Wilmette, Illinois.

MOTIVATION AND ATTENTION

To achieve positive results in teaching or improving cursive writing one must make sure that the child enjoys what he is doing. If not, he will write one or two letters in a dull, weary way, and quickly tire of the practice. His attention must be on the form of the letter at every moment.

One way to maintain interest is to have Request Days. Plan no specific letters to teach, but take requests from the floor. You'll probably run out of time before you run out of requests, as the children never seem to tire of it. The class usually practices the letter requested, but if an individual chooses to skip a few that is all right. A variation on the request theme can be to have a volunteer, instead of the teacher, write the requested letter on the overhead projector.

INDIVIDUALIZATION

It is also important that the pupil spends his time on the letters or combinations that are difficult for *him*. This will vary among pupils in a class, so rigid group practice sessions can be fruitless and boring for many, except, of course, for the very useful introductory group lessons.

SOMETHING NEW

Dr. B. F. Skinner, the father of computerized education, has recently developed a new method of teaching handwriting. His series of books is designed to make the child immediately aware of whether his letter forms are correct or not. The workbook has a copy of the letter for the child to fill in. The proper shape of the letter or figure is printed in invisible ink so that correct marks on it appear in gray, and incorrect ones look yellow. A special pen is used. It is claimed that the book is programmed for independent work.*

CHECKLIST

Praise good posture and correctly formed letters.
Use paper ruled for half spaces and dotted top guide, and long
    No. 2 pencils.

---

* B. F. Skinner, *Handwriting With Write and See,* (Chicago: Lyons & Carnahan, Inc., 1968).

Introduce lower case *a, l, b, f, h,* and *k* first.

Practice difficult letters like *f* with dot-to-dot puzzles.

Present *m, n, v, x, y,* and *z* together, as they begin in a similar way.

Review *a* when you reach *d, g,* and *q.*

Teach upper case capital letters next.

Work on easy joinings; then teach *or, os, wr, on, om,* and other difficult combinations.

Use the child's interest in his name to teach that as his first word. Name cards can be an effective reward for good performance.

Emphasize the positive by circling well-formed letters.

Encourage spare-time practicing using the overhead projector, as you watch.

Use wall charts and plastic alphabet guides for the overhead projector.

Individualize practice by keeping class lists of needed practice as you mark papers during the week.

Allow children to demonstrate letters during group lessons.

Keep at least four dated handwriting samples together during the school year, to share with pupils and parents.

Insist on supervised practice if a child is practicing incorrectly, or needs help.

Use sandpaper letters for finger tracing to teach letter form for pupils having difficulty.

Stimulate participation and excitement with Request Days when the class decides what letters they need to practice.

Be flexible and try to individualize as much as possible when introductory group lessons are completed.

12

How to Keep Oral Reading
from Being a Bore

There are few things as monotonous as listening to someone read aloud, if he does not do it very well. Oral reading by the typical third- or fourth-grade reader is similar in listening value to a sports announcer's description of a baseball game, heard by a person who has no interest in the sport. The voice drones on—the content is lost —all that remains is noise. This is what many of us subject our poor pupils to in the average reading group. Then we wonder why they seldom keep the place, and have such poor attention. Children have a built-in protection against such an imposition. They just turn it off.

We must guard our pupils from this boredom and wasted time, but cancelling oral reading is not the way. Reading aloud is a necessary skill, needed for an entire lifetime, and the fact that it's usually done so poorly points to its need, rather than its elimination. Our responsibility is to provide oral reading practice that teaches or practices the skill without deadening the interest of the remaining pupils.

Take your cue from the special times when children really care about how well they read, and try to make it an occasion for the reader as well as for his audience. This sounds like a formidable task, but it can be done. You can try the individual conference method, and you'll certainly want to make use of all the modern equipment available to educators. Teachers can learn to use these machines and tape record oral reading as an incentive, for its amusement value, and for the opportunities the playback will give the pupils for critical self-evaluation.

Due to the usual urgency of time, oral reading may be shoved aside for other subjects. We'll discuss practical ways to make time for reading aloud by combining it with art, literature, and social studies. Oral reading is just a part of the regular reading skills training, so we can surely weave it into the rest of the curriculum. Since a rehearsal or a play has an urgency and importance that demands a child's interest, investigate the oral reading opportunities in rehearsals and informal performances.

THE CONFERENCE METHOD

To be most effective in expressing meaning, oral reading should be preceded by silent reading of a chapter or a story, and this is usually done in most classrooms. As long as the majority of children stop listening the moment their peers begin to read aloud, isn't it better to allow these bored pupils to do comprehension written work or silent reading at their seats, while you listen to individuals' oral reading? The individual oral reading conference offers the advantage of your being able to focus your attention on one child, rather than sharing it with his wriggling (or dozing) classmates. You'll have time to read aloud for the child as an example, showing how to express emotions. Demonstrate that rate should be appropriate to the material. Pauses can do a great deal to emphasize important ideas. Then when the child reads you'll get a chance to listen carefully and grade him, diagnose his needs, and give constructive suggestions and comments when he's finished. It's probable that you will get around to listening to about the same number of pupils as before, since nothing's been changed except the size of the audience.

READING TO YOUNGER CHILDREN

You may wonder why teachers think it's such a wonderful idea for older children to read to those who are younger, as long as everyone admits the reading doesn't make very good listening. Are we contradicting ourselves? Not at all. A story that can be disastrously dull to hear, read by a classmate after a pupil has just read it himself and knows how it ends, is quite different from the following: A new story is read by an older pupil from a different class. The younger child is ready for something new and different, and the oral reader is geared to do his best. The older one's ego is involved in succeeding in his presentation, so he has practiced it many times, and there is an exciting aura of a performance about his responsibility. The older child will rise to the occasion and try to act it out a bit for his young audience, especially since another teacher is listening too. This is quite a different situation from that in the usual reading group, when the reader couldn't care less who hears him or what they think. He knows they're probably not listening anyway, as pupils all share a similar click-off switch. So, in the reading group the reader drones on, yet when he visits as a guest reader this same child gives a performance. There is a vital factor of motivation and incentive here that makes a real difference.

SAY NOW, PLAY LATER—
USING THE TAPE RECORDER

Many libraries are set up to service small groups of children from your classroom, who may go there to tape record under the librarian's supervision. Then the teacher may go into the library later in her free time to listen to the tape.

To Avoid Embarrassment

Careful planning with your class will make the tape recording session memorable in a pleasant way. Discuss your goals of excellent oral reading without embarrassment with the children, and explain the need for consideration of others. Giggling or teasing could ruin someone's turn. It's important to keep reading groups or parts of the same group together, so that children of similar abilities read at the same time. It reduces self-consciousness, and allows children to read stories at their own comfortable reading level.

Procedure

A story that has been read by all can be chosen, or a new one can be assigned for silent reading. Then, while the group is reading silently, you can call individuals up to assign parts. The best way to accomplish this is to use a class list that was made up ahead of time, with entries like this:

Jones, Mary................top of P. 1 to *down*
Miller, Bob ....*See* to bottom of P. 1

Give each child a slip of paper with his part written on it. He can use it as a bookmark and a reminder. The reason why you need a beginning or ending word written for the half page parts is to prevent children from writing lines in their books. Your master list is necessary, so you can send small groups into the library in consecutive order, or call groups up to record with you. If pupils record in your classroom, they can read alone with you. This list would be needed anyway, as at least three children will lose their parts by recording time. Instruct your pupils to study their parts thoroughly, and to ask for help on pronunciation if it is needed, but to do it ahead of time. Once this preparation is completed, everyone can put the books aside and go on to other activities while the class awaits its turn with the tape recorder.

In case the librarian helps your class with their recording, you have no further responsibilities except to send in your groups in the correct order, and to remind them to say their names before they read. The librarian will play back their recording for each small group. You can listen and grade them later, with the time and freedom to take notes on suggestions for each child.

Don't Overdo It

If you have a tape recorder, with earphones, in your classroom, you can do your own recording if you don't try to finish in one day. Divide the class into four groups and finish two sets at a time. Your pupils will respond if you let them know how important it is to remain quiet during the actual recording. Have a sign ready for the outside of your door, saying "Tape recording. Please do not come in." Assign an interesting written exercise, and make sure that each child completely understands his instructions for it before you begin recording, as you will allow no interruptions. Tell pupils to have in their desks a library book ready to read, when their work is done and checked. Call your first oral reading group up as soon as the tape recorder is ready, and remind them about saying their names before they begin. Write down the number you see on the tape recorder footage indicator, so that you'll be able to find the place on the tape later, and begin. It's better to keep going, with a slight pause between readers as they seat themselves and get settled, than to hear the loud click you usually get on playback when you stop and start the tape between pupils as you record. Some recorders have a pause control, which will allow you to stop recording while you change pupils, without getting this noise.

Playback

When the group has finished reading, give them each a set of earphones, and rewind to the beginning of your recording so that the tape footage indicator shows your starting number. Start the machine on playback, and you'll hear the recording exactly as it was done. Use the volume control to make soft passages louder. This opportunity to hear their own reading can teach children more about speaking distinctly and not mumbling than anything *you* can say. If they have trouble hearing themselves clearly they'll remember this and work to improve their voice projection. Give prompt justice in the case of unkindness to others, and the unkindness won't be repeated. There is interest in listening to this oral reading, because the child has the rare occasion to listen to himself. If you remember, take the sign off your door when you finish.

How to Find Time for Oral Reading— Combine It with Art, Literature, and Social Studies

Due to the urgency to use allotted time efficiently, many teachers combine subject areas when it works well. Oral reading is one subject that can be integrated with just about any other area of the curriculum. These few suggestions which follow should lead to many other ideas of your own.

Reading Follow-ups

One good way to share a book with classmates is for two pupils who have read the same book to work together on a follow-up. They will sign up for a date and time to present an oral reading chalk talk to the class, and the pair will work together to make it interesting and appealing. Their main planning needs some guidance by the teacher, who shows the two pupils how to mark the special sentences they choose to read aloud, with paper clips in the book. The child who will do the drawing needs reminding to make only quick sketches or line drawings with colored chalk, or he'll fall behind his partner. Warn the oral reader to choose only about 15 sentences to read aloud, so that he can hold the attention of his audience. The line drawings must illustrate the sentences which describe them. Instruct the partners to practice privately and to wait for each other so that they will get accustomed to synchronizing illustrations with sentences. The title and author of the book should be on the board before they begin. If the reading is done with the audience in mind, and if the viewers have a chance to see the sketch before the reader continues, this can be an interesting experience for the audience as well as for the participants.

Choral Reading

An activity that many teachers have never tried is the choral reading of poetry. You allow children to become aware of the beauty and rhythm of poetry, while you give the shy child the advantage of a *safe* way to face an audience. Choral reading can be done easily if you have reading groups, by assigning a stanza to each group. Much practice will be needed, but pupils will experience literary appreciation, as well as gain skill in oral interpretation. A good way to present the poem to them is on the lightboard, using the overhead projector. Draw arrows at the end of some lines, connecting two lines that are read as one thought. This will help to avoid a singsong reading approach, which can be very irritating to hear. The children can copy these arrows, which connect single thoughts, on their individual scripts. A great way to showcase the choral poetry is in combination with songs, in music assemblies or festivals. The poem, *Travel*, by Robert Louis Stevenson, is an effective prelude to a program including songs from all over the world, or special music about countries studied in your social studies units.

Plays for Reading Aloud

Your local telephone company has booklets with their Teletrainer sets which have some good plays for third- and fourth-graders, ready to present. The plays deal with communication history and are suitable for large group participation, as they have many small parts. Receiving a part in a play can be a thrilling experience for a youngster, and the necessary practice will be accomplished tirelessly, especially if your group is planning on presenting this production for another class or for parents. It will be necessary to type one dittomaster and run it off, so that individuals will each have scripts. Show children how to circle their parts with colored pencil or ink, so that it will be easy to see when it's their turn to read. Avoid the bother of costumes, but allow the fun of small props. Don't over-rehearse, or your actors will get stale. The main element of good oral reading is full comprehension, so take whatever time is necessary to explain the dialogue and main ideas of the play.

Older groups may be able to write their own oral reading plays. These plays give an opportunity to teach some big ideas from social studies. It's best to work creatively with the informal type of dramatic play, rather than have it read. Each kind of play has its own function and its own value.

Dramatized Radio or Television Broadcasts

This next oral reading project for fifth- or sixth-graders is so unusual that it will be well worth the time spent on it, and it can also develop into a creative writing contest. The scripts which follow teach science and social studies concepts, so you can see that this unit has rich possibilities.

A pupil will play the role of a radio or television news commentator, interviewing persons on the scene of some unusual happening. The scripts will be practiced privately, and read aloud with as much realism as possible. A television receiver may be simulated by the use of a large box with two open sides, mounted on a table. The pupil commentator and the persons he interviews step behind the box and speak as if they were appearing on the screen. The play can be presented as a radio program with just a microphone. The characters in the script are fictional, but the facts presented are accurate, although they do not refer to specific events of a particular date. The two scripts given, plus others written by the class in a later creative writing competition by groups, could be presented to the school as an assembly program. Once the class has heard an informal reading of a few scripts they can be stimulated to try writing their own broadcasts, based on places they are now studying, presenting the typical problems and climate of the regions.

WORLD NEWS ROUND-UP*

Scene: A London hotel lobby

Characters:

Narrator	New York announcer
London announcer	Mr. Lloyd Barton, London businessman
Anne Humphrey, young woman	Mr. R. H. Montagne, meteorologist

NARRATOR: We're going to present to you today a radio broadcast based on events that actually happened in different parts of the world. The broadcast is imaginary and the events described didn't happen all on the same day, or perhaps not even in the same year. But such things have happened and will undoubtedly happen again.

NEW YORK ANNOUNCER: Good afternoon, ladies and gentlemen. It's time once again to bring you our weekly on-the-spot eye-witness accounts of unusual and interesting happenings around the world. This week, nature makes news in a number of different ways and in widely scattered places. First, we take you to our London reporter. Go ahead, London.

LONDON ANNOUNCER: London reporting. People in this city are talking about only one thing today—fog—or to be more accurate, smog. Fog is common in London, the silvery mist that limits visibility to about a hundred yards. Londoners are used to that kind of fog and it doesn't bother them too much, but this is something different. We'll talk more about that difference later. Right now we want to tell you what's happening here. We have set up our microphone in the lobby of a downtown hotel where a number of stranded Londoners have sought refuge. I'm going to let you hear the first-hand experiences of a couple of these people. Here's Mr. Lloyd Barton, who has told me that he's planning to sleep right here in the lobby. Is that right, sir?

MR. BARTON: I don't see any alternative. That's a fact.

LONDON ANNOUNCER: Is your home outside London?

MR. BARTON: No sir. Right in the city. Only twelve blocks away, in fact, but it might as well be twelve miles. Out there on the street you can't even see your feet. I'd be dead lost before I went a block.

---

* Christobel M. Cordell, "World News Round-up," *Colorful Geography Teaching* (Portland, Maine: J. Weston Walch, Publisher, 1954) pp. 155-66.

LONDON ANNOUNCER: I know what you mean. It's even difficult to see people here in the lobby. There's no transportation available, I suppose, Mr. Barton?

MR. BARTON: None.

* * *

LONDON ANNOUNCER: Thank you. And what is your name, miss?

MISS HUMPHREY: Anne Humphrey—Miss Anne Humphrey.

LONDON ANNOUNCER: Are you also looking for a place to wait out the fog, Miss Humphrey?

MISS HUMPHREY: No, as a matter of fact, I'm staying here in the hotel for a few days. I've just returned from the theater.

LONDON ANNOUNCER: You're home from the theater so early?

MISS HUMPHREY: There wasn't much point in staying. No one could see the stage except those in the first few rows. I don't believe even the actors could see each other very well.

* * *

LONDON ANNOUNCER: Thank you. I think you're getting an idea, ladies and gentlemen, of the difficulties people are having in London today. Unfortunately, however, there is a much more tragic aspect to this situation than just inconvenience. All over London people are literally choking to death. Most of the deaths are among elderly people and those with bronchitis or asthma. The doctors have no way of getting to all the people who need attention and the hospitals are already overcrowded. But perhaps you're wondering why this *smog* is so much worse than the usual London fog which I described at the beginning. By a fortunate coincidence, one of the fog refugees here in the hotel is an eminent meteorologist, Mr. R. H. Montagne, and he has agreed to answer a few questions. Mr. Montagne, just what is fog?

MR. MONTAGNE: Fog is a condition that develops when a body of moist air becomes cool and condenses into very tiny drops of moisture which collect particles of soot and smoke.

LONDON ANNOUNCER: But why is fog so much denser and blacker and more persistent at certain times?

MR. MONTAGNE: Usually fog is quickly dissipated by the movement of the air. It takes only a faint current to disperse it. Even if there isn't even a slight breeze, however, fog generally rises into the cooler layer of air that is above it. Then it's high enough so that it isn't bothersome.

LONDON ANNOUNCER: Obviously there hasn't been enough movement of air to dissolve this fog, but why hasn't it risen as you say it usually does?

MR. MONTAGNE: Because at this time there's a rare meteorological condition existing. The air above the fog is not cooler, as is commonly the case, but is warmer. We call this condition an *inversion reef*. The warmer air up above acts like a cover holding the fog down.

LONDON ANNOUNCER: That accounts for the fog hanging on, but why is this fog denser and blacker than usual?

MR. MONTAGNE: Simply because the longer it lasts the more soot and smoke it collects. London, as you know, is a coal burning city. Not only the factories, but probably two million homes burn soft coal. With the inversion reef that I mentioned there is no way for that black smoke to escape, so it mixes with the fog, and we have smog.

*   *   *

LONDON ANNOUNCER: Thank you. We now return to New York.

SCENE: Broadcasting studio, Tripoli, Libya

Characters:
Tripoli announcer   New York announcer
Mr. Lancaster

NEW YORK ANNOUNCER: We go now all the way to Tripoli in Libya, on the edge of the Sahara desert. Take it away, Tripoli.

TRIPOLI ANNOUNCER: This is your Tripoli reporter. Here in this part of Africa the big news is the safe return of a party of American explorers after they were caught in a furious desert sandstorm. The leader of the expedition, Mr. Robert Lancaster, is here to tell you something of the party's experiences. Did any of your group suffer any serious injuries, Mr. Lancaster?

MR. LANCASTER: Fortunately, we all came through the storm in good shape, but it isn't an experience any of us would care to repeat in a hurry. Now that it's over, however, we're glad that we were able to get a first-hand record of the effects of the *gibli*.

TRIPOLI ANNOUNCER: What was your biggest problem during the storm, Mr. Lancaster?

MR. LANCASTER: Believe it or not, one big problem was keeping warm. But the thing that really worried us was that we would lose our bearings when the storm was over. We knew

that these storms can change the whole desert landscape by filling up valleys and flattening hills. Another problem was that in
a sandstorm you feel that you're completely isolated, even in
a crowd.

TRIPOLI ANNOUNCER: How's that, Mr. Lancaster?

MR. LANCASTER: In the first place, we had to keep our
eyes completely covered to avoid the danger of blindness. Until
you experience it yourself you can't believe how that sand can
cut your skin. If it reached the eyes it would be disastrous. But,
believe me, it's a terrible temptation to take a quick look to see
what's happening.

TRIPOLI ANNOUNCER: But why couldn't you talk to each
other?

MR. LANCASTER: Because if a man opened his mouth
he could easily choke to death on the sand he would swallow in
just a few seconds.

* * *

TRIPOLI ANNOUNCER: That's all from Tripoli, ladies and
gentlemen, where the big news today is sand.

NEW YORK ANNOUNCER: Thank you, Tripoli.

Another use for this type of script could be to present it as a
quiz-skit. The name of the place or region involved would be omitted,
and the pupils would be required to determine in what part of the
world the event described took place, using clues read in the script.

In order to develop some good pupil-created scripts, a bit of
guidance is needed. Choose committees, with a few capable re-
searchers on each. Post a sample script on the bulletin board to help
pupils with the play form. Provide social studies and science texts for
each group, and write these suggestions on the board to help the
committees get their own ideas:

> Choose an idea that shows people reacting to some change or
> unusual event.

Suggestions

politics
conflicts between peoples
use of natural resources—not enough or too much
weather event
people resisting a change in their way of life

With the above to start them off, plus a written list of the places
recently studied in social studies, and oral reminders of any unusual

events recently discussed in Current Events, he groups should be buzzing with ideas of their own. The writing will take a great deal of time, so have the committees choose the place, the event, and the characters for the first day's work. They will probably need at least two more sessions to research for facts and write the scripts' first drafts. Individual scripts for each member work out well. Then the group combines the best of each of them into one play. This encourages everyone to contribute. Ask the groups to read the finished scripts aloud for themselves, as a last check on them. They will probably make some changes after this. Have the class organization select a committee to work with you as judges, or draft the class officers, to decide which are the best of the plays. Two out of five should be chosen. The winning committees can select people for the parts and practice their plays to present them for the class. If you have more parts than people, try to include members from groups whose scripts were not chosen. You will have people writing, doing research, practicing reading aloud, and having a wonderful time for weeks.

If possible, obtain 33⅓ R.P.M. recordings of music from the areas written about in the broadcasts. For example, the theme music from the film *Exodus* would be suitable, and very exciting, for Israel, Jordan, or most Middle Eastern countries, as well as for North African countries.* There is a Moslem call to prayer on Side 2.

From this kind of experience the children will develop an ability to work imaginatively, using facts as a framework. This type of dramatization of events contributes to a humanizing feeling of empathy with people of other lands, and gives oral reading practice that everyone enjoys, participants as well as listeners.

WHY IS A REHEARSAL BETTER THAN A LESSON?

We were practicing for a puppet show, and performance time was very near. The oral reading was coming along so well that it was planned to rehearse just the puppeteers during the next few recess periods. The puppeteers were at their places on the stage, and George, a boy who was in charge of lighting, was standing by. I was just about to start reading all of the parts when it occurred to me that George might enjoy reading them so that the puppeteers could

---

* R. C. A. Victor—LOC-1058.

practice. He seemed so pleased at the idea, and he read the parts so carefully and well and with such good expression, that I was amazed. It was especially surprising because this boy regularly had great difficulty reading aloud for me in class, using previously studied material that was much less difficult. The play was too long for him to have memorized it, but he was familiar with most of the words.

The Question

After the rehearsal, as George and I were walking ahead of the puppeteers, I told him how very well he had read. I was curious to get an answer as to why his reading was much better than I had ever heard him do before. So I asked, "George, can you tell me why your oral reading was so great during rehearsal, and you have so much trouble with it in class?"

The Answer

He gave me my answer when he replied, "It's not a lesson."

CHECKLIST

Use every opportunity to improve oral reading skill through supervised practice.

Avoid having your reading groups read aloud by turns unless you can devise a new, interesting way of doing it.

Use the conference method of individualizing oral reading, freeing other pupils for comprehension practice at their seats.

Plan with a teacher of a lower grade for your pupils to visit hers, reading aloud to them and asking comprehension check questions.

Encourage at-home practice just before your pupils visit a younger group to do oral reading.

Motivate slow and average readers by giving them opportunities to participate in the oral reading visits.

Borrow a tape recorder if you can, so that small groups may read aloud and then evaluate their own oral reading skills by hearing it played back.

Emphasize kindness to others, and the urgent need to avoid embarrassing another person.

Keep a record of parts given out for taping sessions of oral reading.

Divide your recording meetings in half if you plan to do them
  yourself, or the proceedings will get too long.
Remind pupils to say their names before they read, to identify
  their recording.
Allow time for silent practice of reading parts before recording,
  and opportunity to consult with you and the dictionary
  about new words.
Integrate oral reading with all other subjects to provide frequent,
  varied practice.
Try out a *short* oral reading chalk talk, using partners who have
  read the same book and who have practiced synchronizing
  reading and drawing.
Plan choral poetry reading for its benefits in speech, understanding of poetry, and practice in overcoming shyness.
Use short plays which have many small parts, to provide an
  exciting way to read aloud.
Dramatize a radio or television script, using an announcer who
  interviews a small group of people at the scene of some big
  news event.
Divide your class into committees, who will research for facts
  and write their own individual broadcast scripts, which will
  later be combined into one group script for each committee.
Select two or three of the best committee scripts and use them for
  another oral presentation.
Give enough rehearsal time and help to make these broadcasts class or school events.
Motivated children work better, so connect oral reading with
  rehearsals for plays and broadcasts, or with stories presented to other classes.

13

Developing A Complete Reading Program

Parents get easily upset about reading. *All* of the language arts are vital to a child for present day communication and future professional success, with good listening getting many votes as one of the most essential. However, none is so charged with emotion as the subject of reading. Just talk to any parent. In many communities it can be considered a heavy blow from fate to have a child who does average work in reading. The tensions transmitted by his family can be added to the pupil's task of learning to read. This possibility points the way to more effective teaching by encouraging a child to relax and enjoy reading, by praising his efforts, and by building confidence whenever you can.

You can do your share in helping parents relax their pressures by not pressing the panic button the moment a child regresses a tiny bit. Try to find out the reason and help him over it. It may be no more than the fact that he didn't like the story you quizzed him on, or perhaps someone teased him before class and he couldn't concentrate. Whatever the problem was, it's the most natural thing in the world for children to learn to read. Put a cereal box on the table before children, and notice how everyone *has* to read all the panels. Just continue making reading lessons as challenging and different as you can, and many of your average and slow readers will bloom.

Reading skills cover an extremely wide range, extending as far as the background experience of each pupil. This knowledge to which the child relates his reading in order to get meaning, can be enriched by field trips, films, television, discussions, and reading. Every vacation experience, visit, or hobby widens a child's perspective and vocabulary in some way, so encourage whatever broadening of interests would be practical for your group's home situation.

This discussion of reading will begin with three complementary approaches which can result in a total varied reading program. The merits of group versus individual phonics teaching will be analyzed and recommendations given. A way of using the tape recorder to ease the teaching of reading groups will be given, plus the writer's opinions on basic readers. A survey of recently developed teaching aids for phonics and dictionary skills and other reading needs will follow.

As Francis Bacon said in his *Essays,* "Some books are to be tasted, others to be swallowed, and some few to be chewed and digested." This comment can be applied to your pupils' reading diet and approach. Encourage them to vary their reading, and teach them to read in a different manner according to a book's value and difficulty.

THREE COMPLEMENTARY APPROACHES TO A VARIED READING PROGRAM

The eclectic approach may lead to a busy year, but it will certainly be exciting and interesting for teacher and pupils. Any method will get stale by spring, but when you divide up your school year between a basic reader with workbook, Individualized Reading of trade books, and a reading laboratory, you will get the best of all three fine reading approaches, and suffer none of the shortcomings which may result from using only one of them.

Is Individualized Reading Enough?

The only good answer to this would be, "It depends on how completely reading is taught with this method." There are some pitfalls to avoid, such as concentrating so much on comprehension and vocabulary that phonics, structural analysis of words, or oral reading are neglected. Another possibility could be spending too much conference time on the vocal few, thereby ignoring many who would be reading without help or supervision.

A careful bookkeeping system will insure fair distribution of your time to all who need it. There are a few children who require some guidance, but who need freedom to work ahead on their own even more. Don't smother these pupils with too many conferences. Generally, the advantages of this reading program outweigh the dangers. Individualized Reading *could* be enough, taught with a carefully structured plan. It is much easier for the teacher, and more interesting for the class, however, to combine it with a basic reader and a reading laboratory.

Basic Readers—Individualized Approach

A difficulty which most teachers are probably ready to mention by this point is that of time, as the basic readers are planned for a year's work. They are well structured, with many extra activities added to a rich and varied comprehension, vocabulary, phonics, and structural analysis program. However, most teacher's manuals themselves say that you need not use *all* of their suggestions. Depending upon the needs of your reading groups, you should use more or less of the material provided, using restraint due to lack of discussion time, and an awareness of a great need for the child to have uninterrupted time for silent reading. The judicious use of teacher's manual material, and the realistic pacing of children according to their abilities and motivation will result in some individuals taking longer than others to finish the reader. Most teachers use workbooks selectively too, choosing only the best pages for required work and varying it for individuals; therefore, children will finish these at different times. Begin with three reading groups in the reader and workbook. After about a month you can let your best readers work independently, with some help from you. Gradually permit the others to work at their own speed, and their motivation will increase.

Grouping

Grouping of pupils for basic reader work is always a difficult task for a teacher. You may use previous reading test results, achievement test scores, and the former teacher's opinions. It is also wise to listen to your group's oral reading and to give them a standardized test, plus an informal quiz, before you decide. A sample third-grade quiz is reproduced below.

> The honeybee family is very interesting. It is a very big family. Thousands of bees live in one house called a hive.

Each bee family has one queen bee. She is larger than any of the others. She is the mother of the hive and has her own work to do. The queen lays hundreds of eggs from which the baby bees are hatched in the hive.

There are the drones who are the father bees. But they are queer fathers, for they do no work. When the babies are hatched in the spring and food needs to be saved, the drones are killed by the other bees.

The workers make up the bigger part of the bee family. They guard the queen, care for the babies, and gather food for the whole family. They not only gather the honey from flowers, but also make the comb in which honey is stored for winter.

QUIZ

1. The largest bee in the hive is the ...*queen*...
2. How many eggs does the queen bee lay? ...*hundreds*...
3. Which of the bees has an easy time? Choose one ...*(b)*...
   (a) all of them   (c) the queen
   (b) the drones   (d) the smaller ones
4. Which is the best title for this story? ...*(b)*...
   (a) The Busy Bee
   (b) A Big Interesting Family
   (c) Where Our Honey Comes From
   (d) Why the Drones Are Killed
5. Must everyone in the hive work? ...*(b)*...
   (a) yes   (b) no   (c) does not say
6. The bees gather honey and store it for food for the winter. Is this correct? ...*(a)*...
   (a) yes   (b) no   (c) does not say

After all of this testing, keep an open mind once your reading groups begin their work. If these groups are flexible, and if you are able to move children from one to another without hurting their feelings, you will have better instruction. Children may try to guess which groups are fast and which are slow, but it is best to never tell them, even if they are correct.

Once you individualize instruction and permit independent work in the basic reader and workbook you solve part of your grouping problems as far as pace is concerned. This is a type of individualized reading using basic texts, so you have no groups except for special needs. The correct book can be the only important point to watch, and never hesitate to switch in the middle of a reader, workbook, or trade book, if it appears to be too simple or too difficult to be worthwhile. The remainder of the workbook can be used in many ways.

INDIVIDUALIZED READING

Since Individualized Reading starts off best with a few people at a time, it is a good idea to follow the basic reader with this system, allowing pupils to begin independent reading in trade books when they are ready, as they finish their texts and assigned pages in workbooks and complete the basic reading test. You may wish to give the basic reading test to small groups, rather than to the class as a whole or to individuals. In this way your slow average readers will enter the Individualized Reading program late, followed by the slow readers who are finishing their work at their own pace, in a different book. Your slow readers will have the stimulation of participation in this too. Fast readers will have more time in the Individualized Reading program, and they will probably utilize it better than the others, who may need more structure and guidance.

Reading Laboratories for Independent Work

The reading laboratories from the various companies all have one goal in common—independent work done at the child's own rate. For younger children they'll give better results if used near the end of the school year, as self-checking and record-keeping require some degree of maturity at each grade level.

TRY VARIED READING MATERIALS

Building Reading Power is a programmed course in reading techniques, specifically designed to improve reading comprehension at or about the fifth-grade level.*

An interesting reading set called *The Literature Sampler, Junior Edition,* is designed to help teachers and librarians encourage fourth-through sixth-grade children to read, and to guide their reading.†
The *Reading Laboratory Series* includes skill-building materials

* Director, Joseph O. Loretan; Reading Consultant, Shelley Umans: Columbus, Ohio, Charles E. Merrill Books, Inc., 1964.
† Dolores Betler, (Chicago: Materials Inc., Encyclopaedia Britannica, Inc., 1964).

that span a number of ability levels, permitting each child to begin at his present reading level.*

GROUP VERSUS INDIVIDUAL PHONICS

During the basic reader part of the school year, separate reading groups and individuals will reach a certain phonics page in their workbook at different times. If the page contains vocabulary words which could be too difficult for a slower group, teach this phonics lesson as a reading group, or individually. However, many phonics lessons are reviews spotted throughout the workbook in sequence, or completely new work, unrelated to daily reading lessons. In these cases it is not economical to teach these lessons separately to groups or individuals. Save time and energy by giving a class lesson and using this written work as a quiz. When you mark these work sheets list the names of individuals who need extra help, and see them as a workshop group on the following day, no matter what reading group they may belong to, or whether they're working on their own. Occasional spot checks on basic phonics concepts will keep the class as a whole moving forward, while individuals who are mixed up get individual help, or small group work. Most labs contain independent phonics lessons, so you will work with separate pupils, but it is still wise to group pupils who need work on the same concept when these needs are diagnosed.

Individualized Reading work seems to call for phonics class lessons, with follow-through's on small groups. The rare cases of children who do not learn with this small remedial group will be taught individually, using extra oral practice and written exercises to be completed at home without help, with checking conferences on the following day. Using group lessons when they are efficient and useful will free you to give individual help when it is needed. If you believe that one or two individuals are not yet ready for the group lesson, excuse them from it by giving them other assignments.

CAN SOME READING GROUP LESSONS
BE TAPE RECORDED?

Please do not skip this section just because you have no tape recorder with earphones. If you start to think how helpful it will be

---

* Don H. Parker, S.R.A. *Reading Laboratory Series,* (Chicago: Science Research Associates, Inc.)

having the tape recorder teach a group for you, you may be tempted to borrow one and try it.

Some suitable lessons for recording would be one containing instructions for children to follow, a short analysis of vocabulary before they begin their silent reading and workbook exercises or a short phonics review. In the case of an oral lesson in which you would ordinarily ask questions of pupils, go right ahead and ask them. Pause long enough for them to think of an answer. Then give it so they can see if they were correct. It works well, and you'll notice children nodding their heads in agreement with your voice. They can be instructed on the tape when to turn it off, remove their earphones, and return to their seats. Select one capable pupil to turn off the machine.

SHALL WE SCRAP THE BASIC READER?

The basic reader has been spurned by many, yet school districts wisely continue to buy them. It is probable that most people who sneer at basic readers as being "boring and namby-pamby" haven't really read them lately, if at all. A recent trend in basic readers is to select and present the best chapters from some of the finest of current children's literature.* This makes excellent reading, and it stimulates pupils to read these books to enjoy more of the same.

Another recent development in basic readers is a linguistically oriented series which gives strong initial emphasis to building word recognition power through the study of linguistic spelling patterns.† Beginning reading is treated as a decoding process, decoding writing, which represents ideas and things in speech sounds.

So, the answer to whether we should scrap the basic reader is "No —not at this time." It is well used as a part of a reading program rather than as the entire course of study, and its use depends upon the class structure.

New classroom groupings will cause changes in the use of these readers. In some multi-age grouped classes doing independent work, the reading group may no longer be practical. In the future, if the

---

* Helen Robinson, Marion Monroe, A. Sterl Artley, Charlotte S. Huck, William A. Jenkins, *Roads to Follow*, (Chicago: Scott, Foresman and Co., 1964).

† Donald Rasmussen, Lynn Goldberg, *The Basic Reading Series*, (Science Research Associates, Inc., Chicago) 1964, 1968.

trend toward independent work continues, publishers of basic texts will probably revise them to make them easier for the child to work with on his own. In the meantime, however, many teachers will devise ways of using these books, giving regular guidance on independent work, or utilizing them as supplementary reading.

If the basic readers go out of use it will not be for the reasons so frequently given. They are modern, interesting, well-done, and many are multi-ethnic, written for culturally disadvantaged city children. The only possible reason for scrapping them or revising them drastically in the future will be the radical new concept of the teacher as a specialist guide to independent learners, rather than an instructor who teaches small and large group lessons.

TEACHING AIDS

One company produces a useful *Corrective Reading Checklist,* which diagnoses reading weaknesses, recommending specific help for them in remedial materials.*

Webster *Word Wheels* are teaching aids for word-analysis skills and individualized remedial instruction.†

A very new concept in teaching material is developed in *Dictionary Skills,* a three level program using transparencies and worksheets for developing skills and understanding in the use of the dictionary.‡ The levels range from early intermediate grades through junior high.

Primary Reading—Vowel Sounds, is a cardboard phonics lesson with attached filmstrip, instructions for the teacher, and groups of words, each numbered from one to ten.§

Alphy's Show and Tell is an overhead projection unit designed specifically to teach the alphabet to primary students, and it provides a basis for any reading program.‖ The package contains exercises which establish correct habits of laterality, listening, and manuscript writing.

Programmed Vocabulary contains step-by-step lesson plans for the

---

* Kottmeyer and Ware, Webster Division, McGraw-Hill Book Co., Manchester Rd., Manchester, Mo. 63011.

† William Kottmeyer, Webster Division, McGraw-Hill Book Co., 1962.

‡ Martha R. Butler, Don H. Stewart, *Dictionary Skills,* Level A, Silver Burdett Co., General Learning Corp., Morristown, N. J., 1967.

§ Clare Fullerton, 1967, John Fraser Associates, Alamo, Calif.

‖ 3M Education Press, Visual Products Division.

overhead projector to improve word power and reading ability.*

There is an almost endless supply of fine reading materials from various companies, most of which is not included here. An interesting set of filmstrips for primary through the upper grades is called *Tachistoscopic Training.*† This teaching device uses a simple attachment for your filmstrip projector called a *Speed-I-O-Scope.* It creates a classroom tool for memory training and improving reading speed. It is used with *Tachistoscopic Training Filmstrips* or *Speed-I-O Slides.* One of these color series is called *New Graded Word Phrases.* The filmstrips are especially useful for tachistoscopic training, but may be used effectively without a tachistoscope.

The *Phonics We Use Learning Games Kit* is a set of phonics games designed to provide experience and drill in hearing, saying, and seeing important basic phonics elements in words. ‡

By Myself accompanies *Finding New Neighbors,* Third Reader I. This type of programmed instruction may solve the problem of using an individualized approach in basic texts. §

A very good series for independent work is the *Reading Skilltext Series.* ‖

The *Macmillan Reading Spectrum* is a complex of instructional materials designed to help individualize reading instruction in the intermediate grades. ¶

CORRELATE READING WITH OTHER CURRICULUM AREAS

In the early grades you can use creative writing as a motivational device to teach and stimulate reading. Plan exciting creative writing sessions for non-readers. They will get the urge to read in order to share what they have written with their classmates. In this way children learn to read through writing.**

---

* Dr. James Brown, University of Minnesota, Dept. of Rhetoric, published by Appleton-Century-Croft.

† Society for Visual Education, Inc., 1345 Diversey Parkway, Chicago, Ill. 60614.

‡ Lyons and Carnahan, Inc., Chicago, 1968.

§ Ginn & Co., Boston, 1963. David H. Russell and others.

‖ Charles E. Merrill Books, Inc., 1961.

¶ (New York, The Macmillan Co., 1964).

** Loretta Doyle, National College of Education, Evanston, Ill.

Our Beautiful America

One creative fifth-grade teacher inspired her class to read extensively for information through an ambitious social studies project.* This study of the United States took from three to four months, and it resulted in a thick book called *Our Beautiful America*, large maps of each region studied, and, most important of all, a class that knew how to read for information, that knew its subject, and was still eager to learn more.

Each student wrote articles covering one of the various topics. Students wrote for their own information to various Chambers of Commerce, the Department of the Interior, and for various travel folders. They learned how to use reference texts of all types, and how to select material from their reading. Class members served as editors and organizers for all materials, accepting only the best. They searched for regional maps they liked, and used the opaque projector to focus these maps on 2' x 3' drawing paper taped to the chalkboard. Three students traced these maps in pencil, went over them later with a felt tip pen, and labeled each part. The hinged covers of the book were painted plywood, painted a bright navy. Screw posts held all papers, and the title was written by using glue covered with red and silver glitter.

EXPERIMENTS

Initial Teaching Alphabet, i/t/a, experiments show promising results. i/t/a contains 43 characters instead of 26, and is planned to teach reading faster and better. Further research results are being awaited.

An automated typewriter can be used in a reading center to teach kindergarten pupils to read. Pupils' nails are painted to match the keys of the typewriter. Children learn symbols and then words. The child types a word and a miniature screen shows a picture as a voice pronounces the word. There is a miniature microphone into which the child pronounces the word.†

PROJECT TO HELP DISADVANTAGED CHILDREN

The Communication Skills Project, *Developing Learning Poten-*

---

* Joyce Arkin, Weber Elementary School, Parkway School District, Creve Coeur, Missouri.

† Dorothy K. Johnson, *New Directions in Reading*, "Experimenting With the Talking Typewriter," (New York: Bantam Books, 1967) pp. 32-6.

tial, is a Wilmette Title I study which began in 1966. It aims to provide comprehensive experiences for a reading background and to motivate the child to read, and it provides reading situations conducive to more effective learning of skills in small groups and in Individualized Reading. It motivates the child to express himself in oral and written expression, and examines the outcomes of written activities as a means of identifying weaknesses in writing skills. Children from homes where only a foreign language was spoken, and hypersensitive, shy or withdrawn children were considered. Pupils whose problems were primarily related to known emotional disturbances and those with severe vision and hearing deficiencies were not included. Project teachers observe and help children in their regular classrooms, but spend more time with them in the project room with learning activities geared to their special needs.*

Changes in School Libraries

Libraries are undergoing a metamorphosis in many districts. One school in District No. 39, Wilmette, Illinois is using its redesigned and expanded library as an instructional materials room and learning center, plus its other functions as a distribution point for books, a source for research, and a place for specialized teaching of library procedures.† Tape recorders, filmstrip previewers, and a film loop projector are used by independent learners in study carrels. A special room with folding doors encloses a television set for class viewing. Teachers have equipment for preparing transparencies and copying. The librarian and her helper assist individuals and small groups who come to read, write reports, read aloud with the tape recorder, or view film loops or filmstrips, in case help is needed.

CHECKLIST

Create a tension-free environment which helps all learning, especially reading.

Extend the experiences of your pupils in every possible direction.

Use three teaching methods in the school year for good results and variety: basic reader with workbook with individual-

---

* Louise E. McKenzie, Director of Project, Principal of Logan School, District No. 39, Wilmette, Illinois.

† Romona School, District No. 39, Wilmette, Illinois.

ized approach, Individualized Reading, and a reading laboratory.

Use varied test results, as well as previous teachers' opinions, if you group for instruction, and be flexible with your groups, avoiding ego damage, whether moving children to slower or faster groups.

Utilize important teaching helps in basic reader manual, but skip material selectively in order to save time for different types of reading work.

Have children begin Individualized Reading experience a few at a time, as they complete basic reader and standardized test.

Use one of the many good reading laboratories available.

Teach phonics efficiently and thoroughly by beginning with group lessons, narrowing small group and individual work down to those who really need it.

Use a tape recorder with earphones for small group work while you teach other groups.

Independent workers may enjoy basic readers as supplementary reading, or may work on their own with regular guidance.

Diagnose and correct reading deficiencies by using tests and teaching aids.

Try the new projectuals, tachistoscopic materials, filmstrips, and spirit masters provided to enrich your reading instruction.

Use creative writing to motivate non-readers.

Correlate reading with all other curriculum areas.

14

How to Teach Individualized Reading –
A Complete Program

Individualized Reading can be personalized for a teacher too. Each individual will use her own methods or variations, and they will work as well as another's. The main ingredients for success in this type of reading instruction are:

1. Remember that it must be instruction. Children can read library books at home without you.
2. Instruct while preserving the joy of the story, as reading can be poisoned by too many interruptions.
3. Maintain a relaxed, but regular, check on reading progress, comprehension, vocabulary, reading skills, and follow-up activities, seeing pupils once during the reading of each book.
4. Teach phonics to large groups, working later on small group and individual needs diagnosed by quizzes.
5. Reading skills require flexible groupings.
6. Sell the follow-up activities by showing them off.

Individualized Reading may be done in many ways, but our discussion will cover some familiar methods. A complete, detailed Individualized Reading program will be presented, giving exact procedures, plus ideas on the use of room libraries versus school libraries.

The question of whether all Individualized Reading books must be read by the teacher will be discussed, as well as how to avoid making reading seem like work.

How I Began

There were the usual misgivings about whether phonics would be ignored, and "How am I going to get around to all of those children for conferences?" and "It's impossible to read all of the children's books in the library," but I proceeded. I had already used one basic reader with workbook in the first half of the year, and a reading laboratory. My class and I were ready for a new experience.

I really had no choice between using a room library and the school library, since I owned about four children's books. The big element of enjoyment in Individualized Reading is a large choice of good books, ranging from at *least* one grade level below to two above your own, to allow for variations in abilities and growth.

After thorough research, thinking of ideas, and planning on the mechanics of the method, I asked our school librarian for help.* All librarians I've ever known have been helpful, but this lady was *enthusiastic,* sharing my plans, and carrying them through daily. She was willing to have my class in individually, or a few at a time, as the books were needed, and to help my pupils with their choices. The main idea of self-choice is not violated when a teacher or librarian checks this reading choice to see if it's too easy or too difficult. Going a little way in either direction may give pleasant reading variety once in a while, but to be a good learning experience, reading books should have interesting plots, be easy enough to understand, and contain new words and good writing to enrich the vocabulary. This superior librarian had been working individually with all of the children in the school up until that time, and she knew them well, but each pupil filled out an interest inventory form which we sent to guide her in helping them. We spoke almost daily about individuals' reading skills, attitudes, and tastes, and the filled-out form helped us to know the children better. It is reproduced below:

Name _____

When do you have the most fun at home? _____

_____

What is your favorite hobby? _____

Any others? _____

---

* Donna Secrist, Librarian, Willard School, District No. 65, Evanston, Illinois.

Name a good movie that you've seen lately. _____

_____

What are your two favorite television programs? _____

_____

What books have you enjoyed reading more than any other? __

_____

What do you like to read about? Underline them, and add others.
    animals   science   make-believe   nature
    covered-wagon days   sports   knights of old
    adventures   trains and planes   mysteries
    everyday stories   funny things   fairies
What person do you want to be like? (in real life or stories)

_____

Make three wishes about yourself. _____.

_____

_____

_____

_____

Make three wishes about school. _____

_____

_____

_____

_____

The pupils were always sure of a pleasant reception at the library, help when it was needed, and guidance in selecting a book of correct reading level, so with this kind of help, the program was bound to go well.

What do you do if you have not yet acquired an adequate room library, or a full-time librarian; or if she is inexperienced, too busy, grouchy, or reluctant? It's more work for you, but you can still go ahead with your Individualized Reading project.

EXAMPLE OF COMPLETE INDIVIDUALIZED READING PROGRAM

Keep the children's interest inventories filed alphabetically in your desk drawer. When pupils return from the library with their choice, have them sign up on your posted conference sheet for a conference. An example of this sheet follows.

CONFERENCES FOR INDIVIDUALIZED READING

_____

_____

_____

Have a signal with your class like an X in front of a name when it's an urgent conference, as when a child wants to start a new book. You skim the book as the pupil sits comfortably. Once you know each child's reading ability well, this may be all you'll need to do in order to see whether the book will challenge without being too difficult. Early in the book it's advisable to have a pupil read a paragraph or two silently, and then ask him to read a few paragraphs aloud. You can probably tell by then whether he can handle it, but give a child every opportunity to change his mind later and return the book if it bores him, if there are too many new words, or if it appears too easy.

It may seem like an overwhelming thought to imagine teaching about 30 children, all reading different books. Try to discover the happy medium between allowing unsupervised reading without lessons, and working yourself so hard you don't even have time to smile at them. This is a matter of individual judgment.

For the benefit of those who have never tried Individualized Reading, the following is a step-by-step description of one system:

1. Welcome the child to Individualized Reading. Let him know that you're both going to have a fine time with it. Give him an interest inventory form to fill out, an instruction sheet, a list of follow-up activities, and a Reading Circle. Ask him to read the instructions carefully, and then raise his hand for a conference with you. The instruction sheet, follow-up activity list, and Reading Circle are reproduced below.

RULES FOR INDIVIDUALIZED READING

Have your teacher or librarian check book for difficulty level. Write your name, title of book, author, and dates you begin and finish book on *two* index cards filled out exactly the same. Keep one card for a bookmark, and give the other one to your teacher.

Write all the words you don't know on your card. Raise your hand for help if you can't find them in the dictionary. Don't skip them.

You will have regular conferences about each book. If you wish an extra conference sign your name on the conference sheet and wait your turn. Write an X before your name if it is very important to see your teacher immediately.

Individualized Reading books will be your desk books. They are not to be taken home.

Check off your Reading Circle to show what kind of book you've read, after finishing it.

Each book must be followed up with an activity that you will select. You will have a large choice of follow-ups, so they should not be repeated except with special permission.

Plan a short follow-up after a long one. Dioramas, peep shows, chalk talks, and dramatized scenes are long ones, because they take time to prepare, and may have to be worked on after school or at home. Some of the short ones on your follow-up list are *a, k,* and *l.*

FOLLOW-UPS FOR INDIVIDUALIZED READING— CHOOSE *ONE*

a. Write a review card. Tell *why* you liked or disliked the book. Name of book and author go on the front of the card.

b. Write a story or poem of your own, using the subject of your book, or any new idea that it gives you.

c. Make a scrapbook of magazine pictures or pictures of your own to show the story or ideas of the book.

d. Draw a picture showing your favorite scene. Name the book and author.

e. Draw a picture showing your favorite character. Write the character's name, and the title and author of the book.

f. Make a colored book jacket from construction paper to fit the book. Write title and author's name on the front. Draw pictures if you wish. Tell a *little bit* about the story on book cover flap, and give your frank opinion of the book on the other flap.

g. Make a diorama of your favorite part of the story, using a box. You may paint the inside of the box, color it, or paste construction paper on it. Combine materials, using pipe cleaners, paper, or anything else to make it look real.

h. Make a peep show out of a shoe box and colored cellophane. This is like a diorama, but it is covered, with a peep hole in the cover and another one in the front side.

i. Give a chalk talk with a classmate who has read the same book. Take turns telling a *little* bit about the story, while the other person draws a *quick* sketch or line drawing on the board with colored chalk. Never tell the ending. Write the title of the book and the author's name on the chalkboard.

j. Tell the main ideas of your story, but stop before the ending and have the class guess what it is. *Don't tell them whether they're right or wrong.* This must be told quickly, leaving out details. It's fun with mystery stories. Write the title and author's name on the chalkboard.

k. If you have enjoyed a funny book, share one *small* part with the class. Write the title and author on the board and read aloud the funny section.

l. If your book has good drawings, share a *few* of them with the class. Write the book's title and author's name on the chalkboard. Mark the drawings you want to show with paper clips.

m. Dramatize a scene from the story with other pupils who have read it. Use the ideas in the book, but compose your

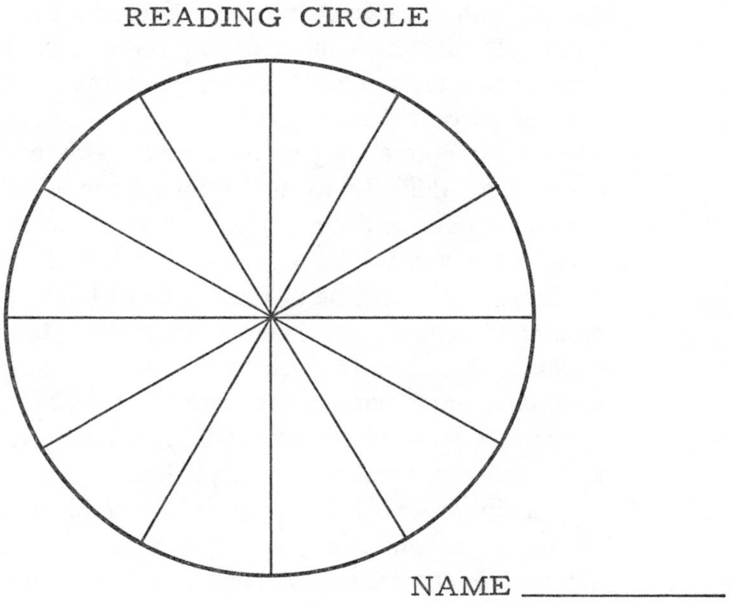

READING CIRCLE

NAME _____

Figure 14-1.

own words after you make a simple outline. Practice the
scene a few times before you perform for the class.

n. If your book is about science, plan an experiment to show
the class. Your teacher will help you with materials. Write
the title, author, and *some* of the experiment on the board.

o. If the book is about collections, start one and tell the class
about it. You can show the beginning of your collection.

p. Make up your own interesting follow-up for your book. Discuss it with your teacher.

q. Plan a flannelboard play, dramatizing a scene from your
book with other pupils. Prepare flannel cut-outs ahead of
time, and take turns changing the pieces. Write title and
author on the chalkboard.

r. Tape record a discussion about your book, playing it back
for the class. Keep a record of number on tape footage indicator.

2. Discuss the instructions, answering pupil's questions. Teach
him to place one check mark in a segment of the reading
circle to stand for one book of a kind that has been read.
Writing in the categories can be a class activity. Get your pupils
started with a few: Adventure, Fantasy, Mystery, Everyday
Stories. If they can't think of any more, add: Humor, Sports,
Animal Stories, Science, Pioneers and Indians, Other History,
Biography, or Other Lands.

3. The child returns to your classroom with a book, which is
checked for difficulty by the librarian or the teacher.

4. When the book is decided upon the pupil helps himself to two
small index cards from a drawer or shelf. He makes duplicate
cards containing: name of child; title of book; name of author;
date child begins book, leaving space for a date when he com-
pletes it. One card is given to the teacher to be alphabetically
filed in a small box on her desk. The other card remains in
the pupil's book as a book mark. It is handy for writing down
as many new words as the pupil finds.

5. The main process follows. It is the child reading happily at
his desk. He will resent it if you stop his reading too often.
Whispered conferences at your desk will not disturb most
children as they read.

6. Post your conference sheet on a nearby door or bulletin board.
Encourage pupils to sign up for reading help, follow-up plan-

ning, or just to talk over the book. If they want to know what a word means, ask them to raise their hands, or get a dictionary, which will save time if you're busy.

7. Answer any questions about words that can be taken care of quickly. Call up the first pupil on your conference sign-up list. Talk to as many as it is possible to do without strain, taking X's first.

8. In your spare time, scan the alphabetical file in your box to pull cards on people you haven't seen lately. A notation of each conference date will keep you informed of this. Pull those cards which show no recent conferences, using the cards themselves as reminders.

9. Expect a card with a finish date when a book is completed. In most cases, schedule follow-up activity before book is completely finished, so that the child may go right on to a new book.

How to Conduct a Good Conference

Ideas for conducting a good conference will come from the child's questions. One may want your help in getting a partner for a dramatization. An announcement may take care of this by locating volunteers. Call first the person on the conference sheet with an urgent X before his name. If you find that it's not really urgent, politely ask him to wait his turn and take the first child on the list. Someone waiting to have a book checked so he can begin it should be taken ahead of others.

Be sure to write a conference date on your index card. The date helps you to check weekly that you're seeing everyone regularly. Notice whether there are any new words on the child's card. If there are, discuss them after a short oral quiz to see if the words were looked up in the dictionary. If you happen to have a question card on file about this particular book, ask one or two of the questions up to the page number where the child has stopped reading. A good question card has a page number for every question so that you don't ask about sections of the book the child hasn't read yet.

Put a small pencil mark under the last question you ask, and file this question card behind his name card in your card box. It's all ready for the next conference. When the book is completed and all of the questions answered, file the question card away. A sample of a typical duplicate index card that a child would fill out is given below:

Jones, Mary

Bees, Bugs and Beetles
Rood, Ronald

Start: 4-10---
Finish: *Conferences*:
                                _____
New Words: 4-12---
_____   4-15---
chrysalis
                                Follow-up:
                                _____
                                book jacket

Figure 14-2.

There may be one more conference on this book before Mary finishes it. You may never get time for it. If Mary signs up for a finishing conference, you can ask her the rest of the prepared questions and fill in the completion date. Mary may change her mind about her follow-up activity, but at the moment she has decided to make a book jacket. It would be much more efficient to just write *f* on her card under *Follow-up*. Most people will not remember what an *f* or a *g* is after a while, so it's easiest to write *book jacket*. Tell Mary that you expect it in a day or two and that she should try to get it in before choosing her next book.

Provide a separate box for completed books on which follow-up's are due, and keep the cards separate, or you might have children who are two or three books ahead of their follow-ups. It may only be because you've forgotten to schedule their book sharing in your plan book, or because you haven't shown them how to make a book jacket. When you have a separate box for these index cards with overdue or due follow-up's they get done quickly because you plan for them. Children need help, supplies, and gentle reminders, or they may forget to do things they really want to do. They enjoy doing follow-up's because of their variety.

If it should happen that a pupil hands you a card with a completion date on it, with a finished follow-up, and if there is no time for a conference, don't get compulsive about the questions you could have asked or the discussion you could have had on this book. The child is almost puffing in his excitement about going to get another book, so this is no time to stop him. The next book will have as many opportunities for you to teach him. He's through with the last one. If you develop this attitude you won't get nervous about all the things you *don't* do. Just concentrate on a tension-free environment, happy reading, and exciting discussions when you listen to *them,* and be content with what you *can* accomplish. Perhaps this is one of the charms of Individualized Reading. You never do completely finish everything or talk to everyone you want to. The children come to regard the conference with you as a pleasant privilege, not a dreaded duty. You may not cover everything in the old-fashioned sense of reading aloud in *every* book, discussing *every* new word, and analyzing *every* plot, but the attitude toward reading becomes happy and intense. The motivating factor alone makes Individualized Reading worthwhile.

You've put check marks after the names on the conference sign-up sheet to show that these conferences have been completed, and no hands are up. This is your chance to take a walk around just to see how the children are doing. One child is working on an index card; another is drawing a sketch of his favorite character for a follow-up, using his imagination and the description in the story.

Conferences with Busy Ones

It's time now to plan another kind of conference. As no one is waiting on the conference sign-up sheet except someone who sees you regularly three times a day, now is a good time to check through your cards to talk to a few who are too busy for you. Call them up politely one at a time, giving each one time to finish the page he's reading if he wishes to. This gives you an opportunity to get the conference date written on the card, and to check to see if you have a question card for his book. In case you have no card, and have never read it, a good conference will result if you ask him to read aloud a bit from the pages he has read. As some type of grading is needed for planning future work, for conferences, or report cards, you may wish to enter oral reading grades on your card at this time. If the card is empty of new words, as most will be, after you have discussed the good points of the child's oral reading, and made any suggestions for improvement, then flip only the pages that have been read, and find difficult words to ask him about. If he doesn't know their meaning and has skipped them, discuss each word's meaning briefly and enter them on the card for future review. If time permits after that, ask him to tell you what type of book it is, and how he feels about the characters. Write down the follow-up activity he has planned, and allow him to get back to his story.

Another child may be called up, but you only have a few minutes. Write down the conference date, and give her a little practice in differentiating oral vowel sounds, as your last quiz showed that she's weak in this. Since your conference time is short, jot down a few words for her to work on by writing whether the vowel is long or short after each word. This practice may be done in spare time later in school, or at home. Have her write her name on the conference sign-up sheet so you can check her vowel sounds with her tomorrow.

HELPING WITH FOLLOW-UPS

Two little girls are eager to practice a creative dramatics scene, but they've been told that it's reading time now and they might disturb someone, so they're working together, writing down a short outline from the scene in the book. These two plan to rehearse outside at recess time. You tell them that if they need suggestions or would like your further help, you're available early the next morning to give your undivided attention. They eagerly nod their heads, and you give them passes to come in early. Your main function then will be to encourage, listen, and remind them to pretend they're the characters and to say what the characters might have said, using their own words. If children get silly, or off the subject, just mention that they don't want to spoil their scene, and then point out the next item on their outline plan. While they're rehearsing, don't try to write on the board and watch them too, as it doesn't work. Rehearsals won't happen often enough to be a chore, and it's fun to see their version of a scene. Pupils will probably want costumes, but limit them to simple props or none.

Workshop on Book Jackets

At the next reading session you may call up a boy who's ready to make a book jacket follow-up and doesn't know how to begin. It's wasteful of time and energy to explain it separately to 26 people. Announce to the class that you're having a little workshop on making book jacket follow-up's, and that anyone who hopes to make one soon may come up and watch, but that you will give another lesson on this in about a week. This cuts the group to about nine, and you demonstrate for all of them. You may wonder, "Why should someone make a book jacket for a book that's being returned to a library?" That's a very sensible question, but our book jacket is another culminating activity to help the child review and condense the story, writing a concise summary of the plot on one flap, and a signed candid opinion on the opposite flap. If a child liked the book in the beginning, but he wants to say, "This was a rotten book," after reading it, let him. Honest expression of opinion is valuable training, and as long as his repulsion doesn't get vulgar, accept it with casual unconcern. The front cover of the book jacket may have a design related or unrelated to the story, plus the title and author's name. However, a neat title and author's name can be enough, without any picture.

After you have told your group what the book jacket will be you might lose one or two in your audience, who suddenly decide that a chalk talk will be easier. Show your remaining workshop group how to fit a piece of 12" x 18" colored construction paper to an average-sized library book. Demonstrate neat folding by matching edges, and using the point of a pair of scissors to score a fold before you fold it. Children will marvel at the sharp fold. Because the book jacket will not be used on the book it really doesn't matter at all if the jacket fits, but why not have them learn to fit it? The pupils should all select their colored paper on the spot and make their folds. Then they can put names on the incompleted book jackets and you'll keep them safe and clean until the children have finished their books and are ready.

It's just as silly to teach the method of making a book jacket to seven or eight youngsters who have no interest in or no intention of making one, as it is to turn yourself into a phonograph record and keep repeating the directions.

The same thing applies to dioramas and peep shows. When one child is ready to learn, demonstrate before a small group. It may be inspiring to some undecided ones (who also have trouble deciding with big menus). Once they see you make something they either have a mad desire to start one right away, or they decide that it's too much bother.

Dioramas

It's a kindness to the parents involved if you confer with the child before he takes his diorama home to work on it. If he chooses to paint it, encourage him to work on it a few minutes before or after school so you can provide the supplies and advice he needs. If he wants a construction paper background, give him a few sheets in the color scheme he's chosen. Try to get him to formulate a plan related to one scene in his story before he goes home. You may have just the thing he needs, like a picture of a window on a greeting card, or a ball of green ruffled-up paper that he can fasten to a twig and make into a tree. Your collage box of odds and ends should be looked through before he takes his project home. Parents usually love to help with ideas and supplies, but they're much happier about it if the teacher has provided inspiration, guidance, a few supplies, and the reassurance that all will not be lost if a rug is missing from the model room. So, between home and after school time, these lengthy projects can be well done without taking away from the child's reading period. If we're not careful, mishandled reading follow-up's could prevent the child from reading entirely. He'd be too busy, cutting, pasting, and drawing. Keep reading time for reading, and entice children into using their leisure time for these long projects. If they're not willing to do this, tell them you'd rather skip the diorama and peep show, as their reading is more important. You have many other activities which are short enough to be accomplished at school.

Diorama

Peep Show

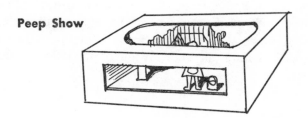

Figure 14-3.

Peep Shows

A peep show is similar to a diorama, except that instead of looking in from the wide open front, you peep in through an opening in the top and one end. These openings can be cut by a parent or the teacher with a razor blade in a holder. The child glues colored or pain cellophane on the outside of the box to cover the holes. When the outside is covered later with colored construction paper, the cellophane-covered spaces for the peep holes will have to be uncovered by cutting away the construction paper carefully. By gluing the cellophane on first, you can hide the rough edges of cellophane around the peep holes with the construction paper.

The completed peep show must be placed in a location near a bright window, or you won't be able to see much inside. Make the holes as large as possible. If a parent is going to cut the holes, mark them with a magic marker. A diorama or a peep show should have a card attached at the side, giving the book title, author's name, and pupil's name.

What do you do with the follow-ups that are made? If you're running out of bulletin board space, perhaps you can string a cord of wire across your room or one corner of it, for a clothesline type display. The pictures will come and go. You may wish to keep the book jackets in your cabinet until an open house or some occasion when visitors will be in the school. They can also be used as a display in the library with the dioramas and peep shows.

BULLETIN BOARD DISPLAY

A dramatic bulletin board display can be made by the class, with some direction from you, using the colorful book jackets. Select a color scheme and obtain heavy yarn to match it. Have a few children measure and put up a map of the world centered on the bulletin board. Choose the book covers of stories which have their settings in various countries, and pin the colored yarn from the book cover to the country represented on the world map.

If you don't plan ahead, you may have too many book covers for the United States and Norway, and not enough for other places. This requires some subtlety. The children are to select their own reading books and their own follow-up's, but there's no rule against having books like the following displayed on your desk, or using any other device you wish to encourage reading books on countries you'd like to have marked on the world map:

Joji and the Fog, by Betty Jean Lifton	Japan
Centerburg Tales, by Robert McCloskey	U. S. A.
Dancing Shoes, by Noel Streatfeild	Great Britain

A committee can be working on letters spelling out a title for the display. *Literature Around the World, Books Around the World, Reading Around the World,* or *Circle the World With Books,* are only a few choices. Just remember that it's going to look mighty peculiar to have a title about *Around the World* and have most of the countries *unbookjacketed,* so plan ahead.

CLASSROOM LIBRARY

The second type of Individualized Reading differs from the first only in the location in which the books are kept. This kind uses a classroom library, which is not as difficult to attain as you may think. There are certain advantages to having your books in your own room. First, it cuts down on the walking back and forth to the library. Second, you can mark the books with grade levels or some secret mark for slow, average, or fast readers, to help you in your evaluation before readers begin a book. Third, over a period of time you can get pupils to write out a few questions with separate answer sheets to be clipped at the back of some of the books as a new follow-up. Try to plan for duplicate books, which are practically a necessity, once the rash of chalk talks and creative dramatics scenes begins, as this is the only way a child can work with a partner.

If you have only a few books, start building a class library for the future, and use the school library in the meantime. If you have a medium-sized collection you can build a library to meet specific needs at no cost by having the group subscribe to any of the fine children's book clubs. One has a selling plan which furnishes the class as a whole with a free book for every five books ordered, if the class is using their company's weekly publication.* Otherwise, you would get one free book for every ten ordered.

Take good care of the books you have, and refuse to allow books out of the room unless a special loan card is filled out. In this way, with patience, with book clubs, and with time, you can build a fine

---

* Arrow Books, Scholastic Book Services, Englewood Cliffs, New Jersey/Pleasanton, California.

library of your own. After all of this, don't get discouraged if many children still prefer the larger choice they can get in the school library.

Do You Have to Read All Those Books?

Of course not, since it's impossible. Many teachers hesitate about beginning Individualized Reading because they worry about discussing books they haven't read. You can use book flap summaries, short résumés from the book club ads, review cards that children have written, and question cards that children or you have written, to make an alphabetized story and question file.

Select a *few* books to read that are so popular they're constantly chosen. These will be such interesting reading that you'll enjoy them too. It's good to be able to discuss with your pupils books that you've enjoyed in common. Gradually build up a set of index cards, alphabetically arranged. Include a short plot résumé or just write a few questions and answers for short comprehension quizzes. It's vital to have a page number from the book for each question. Select a few new words from each book for your cards, as most children will need reminding about writing down new words.

If you skim any book during a conference you can find vocabulary words to ask about, as well as general questions about the type of book. In order to listen to individual oral reading, or to analyze the structure of words in a book, you need not have read it. As time goes on, if you listen carefully to what children say about their books during conferences, book sharing time, and chalk talks, you will become familiar with most of the popular stories at your grade level. Since you are asking the questions, you can guide them in the direction in which you feel most comfortable. It is definitely not necessary to read all or many of the Individualized Reading books in order to teaching reading well.

Reading Skills

Critical reading, structural analysis, (including root words, affixes, and syllabication) alphabetizing, other dictionary skills, reading for information, skimming, outlining of sequence, finding the main idea —there seems to be no end to the vital reading skills our pupils need. It is not efficient, or possible, to teach them all individually.

Try diagnostic pretests and use a large or small group approach where needed, reteaching individuals who need extra help while the class moves ahead. Some skills, like the use of accented syllables, must wait until pupils are ready to master them. Our goal is the child's success, and his constant frustration from having a skill forced on him too soon could result in blocking of learning.

HAVE WE FORGOTTEN PHONICS?

It might seem so, as this is a danger when you're so busy discussing plots, characters, new words, and planning follow-up activities. To give some structure to your reading instruction, it is advisable to plan large group phonics lessons on a regular basis after pretesting, saving remedial work for small groups and for individuals, very much the way you have taught it with the basic reader.

HOW TO MAKE EVERYONE HATE READING

Of course, this is not your goal, but one sure way to accomplish resistance to reading is to demand a book report for every book read. Most of us can remember this old-fashioned teaching method from our own elementary school days. It may not actually make all pupils *hate* reading, but it will certainly cause any child to slow down his reading pace so that he doesn't have to write too many reports. After the first or second book report the slowdown will begin. By the fourth book report most intelligent children will stop reading at school altogether. A few will probably continue reading at home where there is no distasteful required book report. Aside from losing valuable reading instruction, the greatest loss is the child who decides that reading is an unpleasant chore because he associates it with this monotonous follow-up. The use of varied follow-up activities, including so many that are fun for children, precludes this danger. The follow-up's are planned and presented in a relaxed, happy atmosphere, and appear to the child to be a reward for reading, causing eagerness to read more and more.

CHECKLIST

Learn all you can about Individualized Reading approaches, and try those best suited to your methods, library, and pupils.

Try to keep a happy medium between *laissez-faire* Individualized Reading and over-intensive teaching and conference procedures which actually prevent pupils from reading.

Check regularly on each pupil, but don't worry if you are unable to cover each child completely on each book—you can't.

Sell different follow-up's early in the Individualized Reading program to tempt pupils into trying a variety of activities.

Teach reading skills regularly, using flexible groupings, waiting with difficult skills until slow children can succeed with them.

Plan time-consuming follow-up's with your children so that class reading time will not be lost.

Guide children in Individualized Reading procedures with frequent checks and helps to maintain high standards.

Be available for help when it is needed, or very soon afterwards.

Enjoy the follow-up projects with your group, integrating them with oral speech work, art, creative writing, and bulletin board displays.

Plan ahead for your own classroom library, which you can use best as a supplement to the school library.

Read as many books as you have time to enjoy for Individualized Reading instruction, and use summaries and skimming procedures plus pupil reviews and questions for those you cannot read.

Avoid monotony in Individualized Reading follow-up procedures in order to keep reading a pleasure.

Index